THE GOSPEL OF JOHN

PARAPHRASED BY

CHUCK SMITH

ILLUSTRATED BY

RICK GRIFFIN

FOREWORD BY

GREG LAURIE

BIOGRAPHIES BY

CHUCK SMITH JR. & GORDON McCLELLAND

THE WORD FOR TODAY

P.O. Box 8000, Costa Mesa, CA 92628 • Web Site: www.twft.com • E-mail: info@twft.com

THE GOSPEL OF JOHN
Paraphrased by Chuck Smith
Illustrated by Rick Griffin

Published by The Word For Today
P.O. Box 8000, Costa Mesa, CA 92628
Web site: www.twft.com
E-mail: info@twft.com
(800) 272-WORD (9673)

ISBN: 978-1-59751-081-3

Unless otherwise indicated, Scripture quotations in this book are taken from the King James Version of the Bible. Translational emendations, amplifications, and paraphrases are by the author.

PUBLISHER'S ACKNOWLEDGMENTS

The Word For Today would like to thank the following for providing access to original art: Susan and Murphy Graham, Robert Greenwald, Ida Griffin, Deborah Jacobsen, Cindy and Joe Knoernschild, Greg Laurie, Randy Nauert, Don Nuzzo, Charlie Miller, Robert Summers, Thomas and Maria Vegh, and Denis Wheary.

In addition, the publisher would like to thank the following writers and original drafters for their contributions: Greg Laurie, Gordon McClelland, Chuck Smith Jr., Chuck Fromm, and Kerne Erickson.

And a special thank you to The Word For Today Publishing staff.

Layout and design: John Shaffer

F O R E W O R D

IT WAS THE EARLY 1970s when I met the legendary Rick Griffin.

I was in awe of him, having grown up pouring over the adventures of Rick's character, Murphy, in *Surfer Magazine*. Fact of the matter is, when I was an aspiring cartoonist, my little character that I called, "Ben Born Again" was modeled in part on Murphy.

By the late 1970s, Rick had moved far beyond Murphy and the art he was best known for, the psychedelic posters of the late 1960s. Now, Griffin was doing what could only be described as fine art. And even more exciting, he was doing it for the glory of God.

Rick saw things a bit differently than the rest of us, and he brought that vision to his artwork.

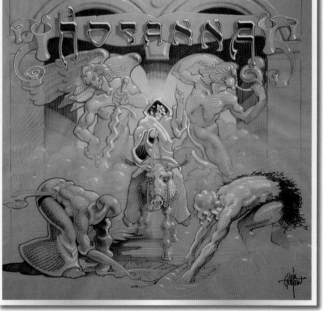

As brilliant an artist as Rick was, he was not always the easiest guy to have a simple conversation with. His brain always seemed one step ahead, giving an artist's take on everything.

I remember one night when Rick and I went to a Mexican restaurant for dinner. They brought coffee to us as we sat waiting for our dinner.

All of a sudden, Rick looked up at me and said, "Greg, what do you see there?"

He was staring intently at my cup of coffee. I looked down with my limited imagination and saw a cup of coffee with the steam coming off the top. The cup was white in color, with a simple design on it.

Before I answered, I looked at Rick, who never broke eye contact with my cup. You need to know that one of Rick's eyes was slightly disfigured from an accident. I always felt that eye made him look more mysterious and even cooler than he already was.

I was afraid to answer. What visions were dancing around in the mind of the master artist? Rick continued to stare down at my cup of coffee in that Mexican restaurant.

I sputtered, "Um, I see a cup of coffee with steam coming out of it!"

For just a moment longer Rick looked at me with that mysterious eye. He seemed disappointed that I had not seen whatever it was that he had seen there in that cup.

It was this "artist's eye" for detail and spiritual insight that gives Rick's artwork its profound nature.

Many have tried to imitate Rick's unique artistic vision, but none have ever come close to capturing it. There was only one Rick Griffin. I am only sorry he left us so soon.

I was thrilled when Calvary Chapel of Costa Mesa commissioned Rick to illustrate Chuck Smith's paraphrase of *The Gospel of John*. What a partnership: a master artist, a leading Bible teacher, and the words of the Book that has brought countless thousands to a vital, living relationship with God.

"For God so loved the world that He gave His only begotten Son, that whoever believes in Him should not perish but have everlasting life."

It is the marriage of Rick's artwork with the marvelous words of John, as paraphrased by Pastor Chuck, which makes this project so amazing and illuminating.

I am so glad that another generation can discover the genius that I believe Rick Griffin was, and to ponder, once again, the intimate portrayal of Jesus that the apostle John records for us in *The Gospel of John*. ✝

Greg Laurie
HARVEST CHRISTIAN FELLOWSHIP
RIVERSIDE, CALIFORNIA

John, Son of Thunder

JOHN AND HIS BROTHER James were sons of Zebedee and Salome, who, some have said, was the sister of Mary, mother of Jesus. It is entirely possible, therefore, that John was Jesus' first cousin. Zebedee's family operated a prosperous fishing business in Capernaum on the Sea of Galilee, and it is fairly certain that they supplied fish to the household of the high priest. Simon Peter and his brother, Andrew, were business partners of John and James. These four were the first disciples directly chosen by Jesus, as He called them to be "fishers of men" (Mark 1:17).

Although John was often rebuked by Jesus for his passionate temperament (for which he was nicknamed "son of thunder"), historians agree that he was the person closest to Jesus during His ministry. Throughout this Gospel, John is referred to as "the disciple whom Jesus loved." Evidence of that love was demonstrated at the crucifixion when Jesus gave His mother into the care of John, the only disciple who had not abandoned Jesus: "And when Jesus saw His mother standing by the disciple whom He loved, He said to His mother, 'Woman, behold your son,' and He said to the disciple, 'Behold your mother.'"

John, his brother James, and Peter formed an inner circle among the disciples and were chosen by Jesus to accompany Him on three important occasions: they entered the house with Him for the raising of Jairus' daughter; they were allowed to witness the glory of Jesus' transfiguration on the mountain; and they were chosen to support Him and witness His agony in the garden of Gethsemane.

After the ascension, the Holy Spirit descended upon the apostles, as Jesus had promised, and transformed them from men, cowering with fear of discovery behind locked doors, into preachers of evangelical fervor who traveled throughout the Roman Empire. Christianity survived and flourished, despite the wrath of an aroused Rome. Persecutions were severe and, in fact, James, John's brother, was the first apostle to suffer martyrdom in 45 AD.

John was arrested during the reign of Emperor Domitian and sentenced to be boiled in oil. Miraculously, the oil did not harm him, and John was then banished to the island of Patmos in 73 AD. But John had not been forsaken. During his harsh imprisonment, Jesus appeared to him in an apocalyptic vision which John later transcribed as the book of Revelation.

Upon his release from Patmos, John retired to Ephesus. There John was implored as the last living apostle to write of his life with Jesus and, under the guidance of the Holy Spirit, he wrote this gospel, three epistles, and the prophetic book of Revelation.

John's gospel differs from the other three in several important ways. Matthew, Mark and Luke chose a biographical form, while John interweaves his own interpretation with Jesus' words to demonstrate that the historical Jesus and the Jesus of inner experience are one and the same. While the other gospels are written as a recounting of events, John, anxious to present Jesus both as the eternal God and as the Son of God, emphasized His humanity as "the Word (Logos) made flesh." Jesus came to earth in human form, but He is divine. "Before Abraham was, I AM." John's purpose was to establish for all time the divinity and kingship of Jesus, and so give Christianity the roots of a living, growing faith. Through John's writing, Jesus calls out to all men to be born anew through baptism and belief in Him.

Because of misinterpretation of Jesus' words at the end of John's gospel, many felt that John was never to die. It is said, therefore, that he merely "went to sleep" in Ephesus at the age of 100 to await the second coming. ✝

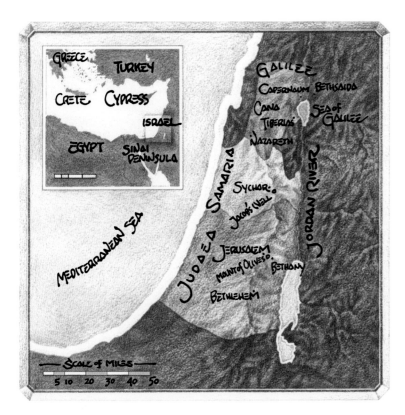

The map shows labels: GREECE, TURKEY, CRETE, CYPRESS, ISRAEL, EGYPT, SINAI PENINSULA, MEDITERRANEAN SEA, JUDEA, SAMARIA, GALILEE, CAPERNAUM, BETHSAIDA, CANA, TIBERIAS, SEA OF GALILEE, NAZARETH, JORDAN RIVER, SYCHOR, JACOB'S WELL, JERUSALEM, MOUNT OF OLIVES, BETHANY, BETHLEHEM, SCALE OF MILES 5 10 20 30 40 50

2,000 Years Ago

THOUGH ONE WITH THE FATHER, the Creator of infinite space, Jesus acted out His public ministry on a very small stage. Aside from His birth in Bethlehem and flight to Egypt when an infant to escape Herod's capture, there is no record that He ever traveled more than seventy miles from His home in Nazareth.

Galilee was the junction of three continents and the meeting place of many of the world's highways. To the southwest was Alexandria, the second city of the Roman Empire; 300 miles north was Antioch, the next most important port.

Across these lands and along its shores passed the armies and commerce of the world. It was a land of strategic importance to the territorial ambitions of Rome, or any other nation, and Rome recognized the necessity for maintaining order in this area.

The land was ruled through a delicately constructed political balance represented on the one hand by the Roman procurator, Pontius Pilate, and on the other by Herod Antipas, ruler of Galilee. Herod's power was constantly challenged by a council of Jewish religious and family elders, the Sanhedrin, whose legislative and ecclesiastic influence was cautiously approved by Rome.

Pilate's official residence was Caesarea, on the coast near what is now Haifa, and he ruled over Judea and Samaria. Herod's seat of government was Sepphoris, near Nazareth; his rule extended over the regions of Galilee and Perea. Pilate's domain was the more powerful because Judah, the center of Jewish politics and trade, included Jerusalem, whose temple was the nucleus of Jewish religion. Here,

then, was the center of the uneasy alliance between the political and religious powers of Rome and the Jewish people.

The Old Testament had promised the coming of the Messiah from its first chapters. At the time of Jesus' ministry, that Messiah was expected to lead the Jews in throwing off the yoke of Roman rule, and those who eagerly awaited this King would readily take up arms and follow Him to this end. But where His followers expected militancy, Jesus answered with love. He emphasized the loving nature of a heavenly Father rather than the traditional concept of a vengeful God of wrath.

Jesus spoke of His kingdom as not of this world. Have any other kings come from such humble beginnings? He chose as His parents a young girl from an obscure village and a simple tradesman, a carpenter. He was born amid the smell and heat of stable animals, and His first bed was a manger. As Jesus grew, He learned Joseph's trade and worked wood with His hands.

Jesus began His ministry with disciples borrowed from His cousin, John the Baptist. He befriended the dispossessed and socially insignificant. His glory was among these, the dishonored, and His greatest miracles were performed for them. He called them to God's army, one of peace and love.

Rejected by His own for not being a militant King, Jesus' ministry still posed a threat to the political status quo of the Sanhedrin.

The stage was set for dramatic events that would alter history. ✝

The Cosmic Word

FIVE AND A HALF CENTURIES before the birth of Jesus, the Greek philosopher Heraclitus first postulated a patterned, regulated universe. Further, Heraclitus stated that nothing in life happens accidentally: everything occurs for a purpose which interacts with every other purpose in life.

The controlling power behind this tapestry of events is the Logos, the Word. Years later, Philo, a resident of Alexandria and a student of both Jewish and Greek philosophy, described the Logos as the thought of God stamped upon the universe. It was Aristotle who arrived at the first principle and final cause of the universe: a pure intelligence, the Logos, the Word. By the time of Jesus' birth, then, the Logos was a familiar concept.

The first eighteen verses of John's gospel are a poem in the form of "Genesis," the beginning. They tell of an ordered universe based upon law or the Logos, the Word. "In the beginning was the Word … " John tells us that the absolute Power at the root of the universe came down to earth in human form: "the Word was made flesh … " The Logos became Man. Jesus is the Logos.

Even before John recounts any of Jesus' words, he establishes Jesus' duality as God and human. Throughout the rest of the Gospel, Jesus established His own divinity by word and miracle. The essence of John's gospel, the divinity and humanity of Jesus, assures Christians of the intensity of God's eternal love. ✝

In the Beginning

JESUS CHRIST, THE WORD, IS GOD ✝ HE BECOMES A MAN AND WALKS AMONG MEN

JOHN THE BAPTIST PREPARES THE PEOPLE FOR CHRIST'S SPIRITUAL MISSION PREDICTED BY THE PROPHETS

CHAPTER ONE

In the beginning

WAS THE WORD, who is Jesus, and the Word was with God, and the Word was God. He existed in the very beginning with God. Everything in the universe was created by Him. He is the creative Force behind everything that has been created. In Him is life and this life is the Light of men. His light came to shine in the darkness of this world, but the dark minds of men did not understand Him.

God sent a man named John to witness that Jesus is the Light, that through His witness all men might believe. John was not the Light, but only a witness of the Light.

Jesus is the true Light for every man in the world. He came into this world which He created, and though He was the very Creator of man, they failed to recognize Him.

When He came to His own people, they didn't receive Him. But to those who will receive Him, He gives the authority and power to become children of God; they are children, who are born not of blood, nor of the will of man's flesh, but of God.

Jesus, the Word, became flesh and settled down and made His home among us. We saw His glory, the glory of the only begotten Son of God, who is full of grace and truth. John the Baptist introduced Him, saying, "This is the One I was telling you about. Though He has come here after me, He ranks before me, for He existed before me. He has shared rich blessings with all of us, for the law was given by Moses, but forgiveness and truth have come to us by Jesus Christ. No man has seen God at any time, except God's only begotten Son who was there with His Father. Now Jesus has manifested God to us."

When the Jews sent priests and Levites from Jerusalem to ask him who he was, this was the answer that John gave to them. He openly answered their questions, not trying to dodge the issues, and declared, "I am not the Messiah." So they asked him, "Who are you then? Are

"I am the voice of one crying in the wilderness, 'Make straight the way for the Lord.'" JOHN 1:23

you Elijah?" He said, "No." They then asked, "Are you the Prophet?" Again he answered, "No." So they plainly asked him, "Who are you? We have to give an answer to the people who have sent us. What do you say of yourself?" John said, "I am the voice of one crying in the wilderness, 'Make straight the way for the Lord,' as the prophet Isaiah foretold."

Those who had come to John were of the sect of the Pharisees, so they asked him, "Why are you baptizing then, if you are not the Messiah, or Elijah, or the other Prophet?" John answered them, "I am baptizing with the two disciples of John heard him declare this, they began to follow Jesus. He turned and saw them following Him, and said to them, "Who are you looking for?" They said to Him, "Rabbi (which is interpreted Master), where do You live?" He said to them, "Come and see." So they went with Him and saw where He was living and they stayed with Him that day, for it was about four o'clock in the afternoon. One of the two who heard John speak and followed after Jesus was Andrew, who was the brother of Simon Peter. Andrew went to find his brother and told him, "We have found the Messiah" (which interpreted into Greek is "the

Look, this is the Lamb of God
who takes away the sins of the world!

water, but there is One who is standing among you whom you do not know. He is the One who is coming after me, who has been preferred before me, and I am not worthy to tie His shoelaces." These things happened near the city of Bethabara, in the area of the Jordan River where John was baptizing.

The next day as John saw Jesus coming to him, he said, "Look, this is the Lamb of God who takes away the sins of the world! This is the One I was telling you about who was coming after me but was preferred before me. I have come baptizing with water in order to make Him known to Israel."

Then John said, "I saw the Spirit descending from heaven like a dove and it rested on Him. I did not realize that He was the Messiah until this happened, for the One who sent me to baptize with water said to me, 'The One upon whom you see the Spirit of God descending and remaining is the One who will baptize with the Holy Spirit.' And I saw the dove and I declare the truth, that this is the Son of God."

On the following day John was standing with two of his disciples, and when they saw Jesus walking by, John declared, "Look, the Lamb of God." When

Christ"). He brought Simon Peter to Jesus and when Jesus looked at him, He said, "You are Simon, the son of Jonah, but you shall be called Peter" (which means "a little stone").

The next day as Jesus was going to Galilee, He found Philip and He said to him, "Follow Me." Philip was from Bethsaida, the same hometown of Andrew and Peter. Philip in turn found Nathanael and said to him, "We have found Him, whom Moses wrote about in the law and who was prophesied by the prophets, Jesus of Nazareth, the Son of Joseph." Nathanael answered him, "Can any good thing come out of Nazareth?" Philip said, "Come and see." When Nathanael came to Jesus, Jesus said of him, "Here is an Israelite in whom there is no deceit." Nathanael said, "How do You know me?" Jesus answered him and said, "Before Philip called you, when you were under the fig tree, I saw you." Nathanael answered Him, "Rabbi, You are the Son of God, You are the King of Israel." Jesus said to him, "Because I said to you I saw you under the fig tree, do you believe? You're going to see greater things than this. I tell you the truth, after these things you are going to see the heavens open and the angels of God ascending and descending upon Me." ✝

Water to Wine

JESUS MIRACULOUSLY CHANGES ORDINARY WATER INTO EXTRAORDINARY WINE AT A WEDDING CELEBRATION

† JESUS THROWS OUT THE MERCHANDISERS FROM THE TEMPLE IN JERUSALEM

CHAPTER TWO

WATER TO WINE

HREE DAYS LATER Jesus was at a wedding in Cana. The mother of Jesus was also attending, along with His disciples. When they ran out of wine, Jesus' mother came to Him and said, "They have no wine." Jesus answered her, "What are you trying to do to Me? My hour has not yet come." But the mother of Jesus said to the servants, "Whatever He tells you to do, do it."

There were six large waterpots made of stone there, the type used by the Jews for purifying purposes. They each held approximately twenty gallons.

Jesus said to the servants, "Fill the waterpots with water." So they filled them to the brim. He then said to them, "Draw now out of the waterpots and take some to the ruler of the feast." So they carried it to the ruler of the feast. When the ruler tasted the water that was made into wine and did not know where it had come from (but the servants which had drawn the water knew), he called the bridegroom and said to him, "Usually at the beginning of the feast you serve the good wine, and when people are full, then you bring out your cheaper wine. But you have kept the good wine until now."

This was the beginning of the miracles which Jesus did in Cana of Galilee, as He began to manifest His glory. And His disciples believed in Him.

After this He went down to Capernaum with His mother and His brothers and His disciples, but they did not remain there very long, for the Jews' Passover was approaching and Jesus wanted to be in Jerusalem for the Passover.

When He arrived in Jerusalem, He found in the temple those who were selling oxen and sheep and doves, and those who were exchanging money in the temple

Jesus said to the servants, "Fill the waterpots with water." So they filled them to the brim. **JOHN 2:7**

This was the beginning of the miracles which Jesus did in Cana of Galilee, as He began to manifest His glory.

And His disciples believed in Him.

precincts. So He made a whip from small cords, and He drove them all out of the temple along with their sheep and oxen, and overturned the money changers' tables, dumping the money on the floor. And He said to those who were selling doves, "Take these things out of here. Do not make My Father's house a house of merchandise." And His disciples remembered the prophecy from the Scriptures that declared, "Concern for God's house will be My chief concern."

Then the Jews asked Him, "What sign will You show us to prove You have authority to be doing these things?" Jesus answered them, "Destroy this temple and in three days I will rebuild it." Then the Jews answered Jesus, "We've been building this temple for forty-six years, and You mean to say You will rebuild it in three days?" But Jesus was speaking of the temple of His body. And after He was risen from the dead His disciples remembered that He had said this to them, and they believed the Scripture and the word which Jesus had said. When He was in Jerusalem at the Passover, on the feast day, many believed He was the Messiah when they saw the miracles that He did. But Jesus would not trust them, because He knew all men. He did not need anyone to tell Him about men, for He knew the inner secrets of men. ✝

He then said to them, "Draw now out of the waterpots and take some to the ruler of the feast." **JOHN 2:8**

Midnight Interview

NICODEMUS, AN ELDERLY JEWISH MINISTER, SECRETLY INTERVIEWS JESUS †
JESUS TELLS HIM ABOUT SPIRITUAL REBIRTH † JOHN THE BAPTIST EXPLAINS SPIRITUAL THINGS TO HIS LISTENERS

CHAPTER THREE

HERE WAS A MAN who was a Pharisee, whose name was Nicodemus. He was a ruler of the Jews. One night he came to Jesus and said to Him, "Rabbi, we know that You are a teacher and that You are from God, for no man can do the miracles that You are doing unless he is from God." Jesus answered him, "I will tell you an important truth: unless a man is born again, he cannot see the kingdom of God." Nicodemus said to Him, "But how can a man be born when he is old? Can he re-enter his mother's womb and be born?" Jesus answered, "The truth is that unless a man is born of water and of the Spirit, he cannot enter into the kingdom of God. For that which is born of flesh is flesh, and that which is born of the Spirit is spirit. Don't be surprised that I said you must be born again. The wind blows wherever it wishes, and you can hear the sound of it, but you cannot tell where it has come from or where it is going. So it is with everyone that is born of the Spirit." Nicodemus answered, "How can these things be?" Jesus said, "Are you a teacher of the Israelites and you do not know these things? I tell you the truth. I know the things I am talking about, for I have seen them; yet you do not receive My declarations. If I have told you of things that pertain to the earth and you do not believe, then how will you believe if I tell you of the things that pertain to heaven? No man has ascended into heaven but Me, the One that came down from heaven. And even as Moses lifted up the serpent on a pole in the wilderness, even so must the Son of Man be lifted up, that whosoever will believe in Him should not die, but will have eternal life."

"For God so loved the world that He gave His only Son, that whoever believes in Him should not die, but have everlasting life. For God did not send His Son into the world to condemn the world, but to save the world through Him. Whoever trusts in Him is not condemned, but whoever does not believe is already condemned, because he has not trusted in the only Son of God."

"And this is the condemnation: that light came into the world and men loved darkness rather than the light because their deeds were evil. Everyone who does evil hates the light, for it reveals his evil deeds. He that is walking in truth welcomes the light because it reveals that he is doing God's will."

After these things, Jesus went with His disciples to Judea and stayed there with them as they baptized.

And even as Moses lifted up the serpent on
a pole in the wilderness, even so must the
Son of Man be lifted up.

JOHN 3:14

For God so loved
the world that He gave His only Son, that whoever believes in Him should not die, but have everlasting life.

◆

John was also baptizing in Aenon, near Salim, because of the abundance of water there, and people came and were baptized. At this time John was not yet put in prison. Then there arose a question between some of John's disciples and the Jews about their purification rites. And they came to John and said to him, "Rabbi, He who was with you on the other side of Jordan, whom you declared to be the Son of God, is also baptizing and many are coming to Him." John answered, "A man can receive nothing unless it is given to him from heaven. You know that I told you I am not the Christ, but that I was sent before Him. The bride belongs with the Bridegroom, but the friend of the Bridegroom, who stands and helps Him, rejoices greatly when he hears the Bridegroom's voice. My joy therefore is complete. He must increase and I must decrease."

"He that came from heaven is above all, but he that is of earth is earthly and speaks of the things of the earth. He has declared the things which He has seen and heard, but few will accept His testimony. Those who have accepted His testimony that God is true, will swear to it for the One whom God has sent speaks the words of God. For God has not

given Him just a measure, but the fullness of the Spirit. The Father loves His Son and has placed all things in His hands. Whoever believes in the Son has everlasting life, but those who do not believe in the Son will not have life, for the wrath of God is resting on them." ✝

Drink of Eternity

JESUS REVEALS THE SPIRITUAL TRUTH TO A PROMISCUOUS WOMAN † HE MIRACULOUSLY HEALS A MAN'S SON FROM NEAR-FATAL SICKNESS

CHAPTER FOUR

HEN THE LORD knew that the Pharisees had heard that He was baptizing more new believers than John (although Jesus was not baptizing but His disciples were), He left Judea with His disciples and went to Galilee. On the journey it was necessary that they travel through Samaria. Thus, they came to a Samaritan city called Sychar, which was near the lot that Jacob had given to his son Joseph. They stopped at Jacob's well because Jesus was weary from traveling. It was the sixth hour. The disciples went into the city to buy supplies and Jesus remained at the well. When a woman of Samaria came to the well to draw water, Jesus said to her, "May I have a drink?" The woman of Samaria said to Him, "Why do You ask me for a drink since You are a Jew and I am from Samaria? The Jews will not deal with the Samaritans." Jesus answered her, "If you knew the gift of God and who it was that said to you, 'Give Me a drink,' you would have asked Him and He would have given you living water." The woman said to Him, "Sir, You do not have anything to draw water with and this well is deep. Just where are You going to get this water? Are You greater than our father Jacob, who gave us this well

and drank from it himself, as well as his children and cattle?" Jesus said, "Whoever drinks this water will thirst again, but whoever drinks the water that I will give him will never thirst again. But the water that I shall give will be like a well of water springing up to everlasting life." The woman said, "Give me some of this water so that I will not thirst, and I won't have to come here to draw water again." Jesus said to her, "First go and call your husband to come." The woman answered, "I don't have a husband." Jesus said, "That's true when you say, 'I don't have a husband,' for you've had five husbands and the man you're living with now is not your husband."

The woman said to Him, "Sir, I perceive that You are a prophet. Our fathers worshiped in this mountain, but you Jews say that Jerusalem is the place where men have to worship God." Jesus said to her, "Woman, believe Me, the hour is coming when you will neither worship God in this mountain nor at Jerusalem. You Samaritans do not know whom you are worshiping. We know whom we worship, for salvation is coming through the Jews. The time has come when the true worshipers of the Father will worship Him in Spirit and truth. God is a Spirit and those that worship Him must worship Him in spirit and truth." The woman said to

Whoever drinks this water will thirst again, but whoever drinks the water that I will give him will never thirst again. **JOHN 4:13-14**

Him, "I know that the Messiah is coming, who is called the Christ. And when He comes He is going to tell us everything." Jesus said to her, "I, the One speaking to you, am He."

At this time the disciples came and they were amazed that He was talking with the woman, yet none of them said to Him, "What's going on?" or "Why were You talking to her?" And the woman left her waterpot and

more believed in Him when they heard His words. And they said to the woman, "Now we believe, not because of what you told us, but because we have heard Him ourselves and we know that He is really the Christ, the Savior of the world."

After two days He left there and went to Galilee. Jesus often said that a prophet has no honor in his own country, but when He reached Galilee, the Galileans

The water that I shall give will be like a well of water, springing up to everlasting life.

went into the city and said to the men, "Come and see a Man who told me everything I ever did. Isn't this the Messiah?" Then they went to Jesus. In the meantime, the disciples said to Him, "Master, You'd better eat." But He said to them, "I have meat to eat that you do not know about." The disciples said to each other, "Has someone brought Him something to eat?" Jesus said, "My meat is to do the will of Him Who sent Me, and to finish His work. Do not say that there are four months and then the harvest will come. I say to you, look up, look at the fields for they are ready to harvest now. Those who reap will receive wages, and they will gather the fruit of life eternal. Those who sow and those who reap will rejoice together. This is a true saying: one sows and another reaps. I send you to reap the harvest that you did not sow. Other men have worked and you will reap the fruit of their labors."

Many of the Samaritans from that city believed in Him because of the testimony of the woman who said, "He told me everything that I have ever done." So when the Samaritans had come to Him, they begged Him to stay with them. He stayed there for two days, and many

received Him because they had seen all the things He did at Jerusalem, at the feast, for they had gone to the feast also.

Jesus returned to Cana of Galilee where He had made the water into wine. There was a certain nobleman whose son was sick at Capernaum. When he heard that Jesus had come from Judea back into Galilee, he went to Him and begged Him to come down and heal his son, for he was almost dead. Then Jesus said to him, "Unless you see signs and wonders, you will not believe." But the nobleman said to Him, "Sir, please come down or my child will die." Jesus said to him, "You may go on your way for your son will live." And the man believed what Jesus told him and he went on his way. While he was traveling, his servants met him and told him, "Your son is alive." He asked them at what hour his son began to get better. They said, "Yesterday at one o'clock in the afternoon the fever broke." The father knew that it was at the same hour that Jesus said to him, "Your son will live." He believed and his whole household also believed. This is the second miracle which Jesus did when He returned from Judea to Galilee. ✝

Lame Man Healed

A CRIPPLED MAN IS MIRACULOUSLY HEALED BY CHRIST † THE JEWISH LEADERS PERSECUTE JESUS FOR IGNORING THEIR RELIGIOUS RULES.
THEN PLAN TO KILL HIM FOR CLAIMING TO BE EQUAL WITH GOD

CHAPTER FIVE

FTER THIS, there was a Jewish feast and Jesus went back to Jerusalem. In Jerusalem, by the sheep market, was a pool (which in Hebrew is called "Bethesda") and it had five porches. In these porches a great crowd of lame and blind and sick people would lie, waiting for the waters to move. For an angel would go down to the pool at a certain time and would stir the water, and whoever was the first to get into the water after it had been stirred was healed from whatever disease he had. There was a certain man there who had suffered an illness for thirty-eight years. When Jesus saw him lying there and knew that he had been sick a long time, He said to him, "Would you like to be healed?" The lame man answered Jesus, "Sir, I do not have anyone to help me into the water when it is stirred, for while I'm trying to get in, someone always steps in before me." Jesus said to him, "Stand up and take up your bed and walk." Immediately the man was healed, and he picked up his bed and walked.

Then the Jews said to the man who was healed, "It's the Sabbath day and it is not lawful for you to carry your bed." He answered them saying, "The One who healed me told me to take up my bed and walk." Then they asked him, "Who is the One who told you to take up your bed and walk?" The man who was healed could not answer them for he did not know who He was, for Jesus had moved on with the crowd that was in that place. Later Jesus found the man in the temple and said to him, "You have been healed. Do not sin again, or else a worse thing may come upon you." The man went and told the Jews that it was Jesus who had healed him. So the Jews began to persecute Jesus, and they made plans to kill Him because He had done these things on the Sabbath day. But Jesus answered them, "My Father works on the Sabbath day and so do I." Therefore the Jews wanted all the more to kill Him, because He had not only broken the Sabbath day law, but He said that God was His Father, and He was continually claiming to be equal with God.

So Jesus answered and said to them, "I tell you the truth, the Son can do nothing by Himself, but only those things which He sees the Father do. For whatever things the Father does, the Son does also. For the Father loves the Son and shows Him everything that He does. And He will show even greater works than these, so that you will be astounded. For as the Father raises up the dead and gives them life, even so the Son gives life to whom

For as the Father raises up the dead and gives them life, even so the Son gives life to whom He is pleased to give it. JOHN 5:21

He is pleased to give it. Moreover, the Father judges no one, but has committed all judgment to the Son so that all men will honor the Son, even as they honor the Father. He who does not honor the Son does not honor the Father who sent Him. I tell you the truth: he who hears My word and believes in Him who sent Me has everlasting life and will not come into condemnation, but has passed from death into life. I tell you the truth: the hour is coming when the dead shall hear the voice of Me are true. You have gone out to listen to John's preaching and he told you the truth. The truest witness of Me is not John, but I am saying these things that you might be saved. For John was a burning and shining light, and you were willing to rejoice in his light for a while. But I have a greater witness than John: the works which the Father has given Me to finish. These works that I do prove that the Father has sent Me. But you have neither heard His voice at any time nor seen

---

He who hears My word and believes in Him who sent Me has everlasting life and will not come into condemnation, but has passed from death into life.

---

of the Son of God and those who hear will live. For as the Father has life in Himself, so has He given power to the Son to have life in Himself and has given Him authority to execute judgment because He is the Son of Man."

"Do not marvel at this, for the hour is coming when all of those who are in the graves shall hear His voice, and they shall come forth: those who have done good to the resurrection of life, and those who have done evil to the resurrection of death and damnation. I cannot do anything by Myself, but as I hear I judge, and My judgment is fair because I do not seek to do My own will but to do the will of the Father who sent Me."

"If I witnessed of Myself, you would not accept My witness as true. But there is another who witnesses of Me, and I know that the things that He is witnessing

His form. And you do not have His word abiding in you, for you have not believed the One whom He sent."

"You search the Scriptures because in them you think that you have eternal life, but they are actually witnessing of Me. You will not come to Me to receive life. I do not receive honor from men, for I know that you do not have the love of God in you. I have come in My Father's name and you do not accept Me. Another one is coming in his own name and you will receive him. How can you believe what I say when you receive honor from each other and you do not care about the honor which comes only from God? Do not think that I will accuse you before the Father for there is another who accuses you, even Moses, the one you trust in. If you had believed Moses, you would have believed Me, for he wrote of Me. But if you do not believe his writings, how will you believe My word?" ✝

Wonder Bread

JESUS MIRACULOUSLY FEEDS A CROWD OF 5,000, BUT THE PEOPLE FAIL TO UNDERSTAND THE SPIRITUAL SIGNIFICANCE ✝ THAT NIGHT HIS DISCIPLES
CROSS THE LAKE BY BOAT ✝ JESUS COMES TO THEM BY WALKING ON THE WATER

CHAPTER SIX

FTER THESE THINGS Jesus went over the Sea of Galilee, which is also called the Sea of Tiberias. A great crowd of people followed Him because they had seen the miracles He did for those who were diseased. Jesus went up into a mountain and He sat with His disciples. It was close to the time of the Feast of Passover and Jesus saw a great multitude of people coming to Him, so He said to Philip, "Where can we buy some bread for these people?" He said this to test Philip, for He knew what He was going to do. Philip answered Him, "If we had $3,000 worth of bread, it probably wouldn't be enough to give everyone just a little." One of His disciples, Andrew (who was Simon Peter's brother), said to Him, "There's a little boy here who has five barley loaves and two small fish, but this could not possibly serve so many people." Jesus said, "Have the men sit down." This was a very grassy area, so the men sat down—about five thousand in all. Jesus took the loaves, and after He had given thanks, He gave them to the disciples, and the disciples distributed them to those who were sitting down. He did the same with the fish, so that they ate as much as they desired. When they were all filled, He said to His disciples, "Gather up the fragments that remain, so that we won't waste anything." From the five barley loaves and two fish, they gathered twelve baskets of fragments which remained beyond all that had been eaten.

When the men saw the miracle that Jesus did, they said, "This is surely the Prophet who is to come into the world."

When Jesus perceived that they were planning to come and take Him by force to make Him their King, He departed from there and went alone to a mountain. When evening came, His disciples went down to the sea. They entered a ship and went over the sea toward Capernaum, for it was dark and Jesus had not yet come to them. Then a great wind began to blow, creating a rough sea. When they had rowed two or three miles, they saw Jesus walking toward them on the sea and they were frightened. As He was coming near the ship He said, "Don't be afraid, it's Me." Then they willingly received Him into the ship and immediately the ship was at the land where they were going.

The next day the people who had remained on the other side of the sea knew that there had been only one boat there, and that Jesus had not entered that boat with His disciples, but that the disciples had gone away alone. (However, there were many other boats that came from Tiberias and landed near the place where they ate bread after the Lord had given thanks.) When the people saw that Jesus was not there and neither were His disciples, they also took ships and they went to Capernaum looking for Jesus. When they found Him on the other side of the sea, they said, "Rabbi, how did You get here?" Jesus answered them saying, "I tell you the truth: you were not looking for Me

They saw Jesus walking toward them on the sea and they were frightened. **JOHN 6:19**

because you saw miracles, but because you ate the loaves and were filled. Don't labor for the food that perishes, but for the food that endures to everlasting life, which the Son of Man shall give to you, for God the Father has approved Him."

Then they asked Him, "What shall we do so that we might do the works of God?" Jesus answered them, "This is the work of God: just believe on the One He has sent." They asked Him, "What sign will You show us then, that we might see it and believe You? What work will You do? For our fathers ate manna in the desert and it is written, 'He gave them bread from heaven to eat.'" Then Jesus said to them, "I will tell you the truth: Moses

the truth: he who believes on Me has everlasting life. I am that Bread of life. Your fathers ate the manna in the wilderness and are dead. I am the living Bread, which came down from heaven, and if any man will eat this Bread, he will live forever. The bread that I will give is My flesh which I will give for the life of the world."

The Jews therefore had arguments among themselves, saying, "How can this Man give us His flesh to eat?" Then Jesus said to them, "I tell you the truth, unless you eat the flesh of the Son of Man and drink His blood, you do not have life. Whoever will eat My flesh and drink My blood has eternal life and I will raise him up at the last day. For My flesh is the bread and My blood is drink, and he who

—— Don't be afraid. It's Me. ——

did not give you that bread from heaven, but My Father gave you the true bread from heaven. For the Bread of God is He who came down from heaven to give life to the world." Then they said to Him, "Lord, continually give us this eternal life." Jesus said to them, "I am the Bread of life, and he who comes to Me shall never hunger, and he who believes on Me shall never thirst. But as I said to you, you have seen Me and did not believe. All those that the Father gives Me shall come to Me, and anyone who comes to Me I will never reject. For I did not come from heaven to do My will, but the will of Him who sent Me. And this is My Father's will who sent Me: that I should not lose one of those whom He has given to Me, but that I should raise them up in the last day. This also is the will of Him who sent Me: that everyone who sees the Son and believes on Him may have everlasting life, and I will raise him up at the last day."

The Jews then murmured against Him because He said, "I am the Bread which came down from heaven." And they said, "Is not this Jesus, the son of Joseph, whose father and mother we know? How is it that He says 'I come down from heaven'?" Jesus said to them, "Don't murmur among yourselves, for no man can come to Me unless the Father which sent Me draws him, and I will raise him up at the last day. It is written in the prophets, 'They shall all be taught of God.' Every man therefore who has heard and has learned from the Father comes to Me. Not that any man has ever seen the Father except He who is of God; He has seen the Father. I tell you

eats My flesh and drinks My blood dwells in Me and I in him. As the Father has sent Me and I live through the Father, so he that eats of Me shall live through Me. This is that Bread which came down from heaven, not as your fathers ate manna and are dead. He that eats of this Bread shall live forever." These things He said when He was teaching at the synagogue at Capernaum.

And many of His disciples, when they heard this, said, "These are hard sayings; who can understand it?" When Jesus saw that His disciples were troubled by it, He said to them, "Does this offend you? What will you do when you see the Son of Man ascending to where He was before? It is the Spirit that makes you alive; the flesh profits nothing. The words that I speak to you are spirit and are life. But there are some of you who do not believe." For Jesus knew from the beginning who did not believe and who would betray Him. He said, "Therefore I said to you that no man can come to Me unless My Father causes him to come." At that time many of His disciples turned back and did not walk with Him anymore. Then Jesus asked the twelve, "Will you also go away?" Peter answered, "Lord, where will we go? You have the words of eternal life, and we believe and know that You are the Holy One of God." Jesus asked them, "Have I not chosen twelve of you and yet one of you is a devil?" (He was speaking of Judas Iscariot, the son of Simon. For he was the one who was going to betray Him and he was one of the twelve.) ✝

Wanted and Unwanted

JESUS TEACHES THE THINGS OF THE SPIRIT TO THE PEOPLE IN THE TEMPLE ✝ HE CLAIMS TO BE THE DRINK THAT WILL SATISFY MAN'S SPIRITUAL THIRST
✝ OPPOSITION FROM THE RELIGIOUS LEADERS INTENSIFIES

CHAPTER SEVEN

FTER THESE EVENTS, Jesus was in the area of Galilee, for He would not go down to Judea because the Jews were seeking to kill Him. The Jewish Feast of Tabernacles was near and His brothers said to Him, "You should leave here and go to Judea so Your disciples may see the works that You are doing. No one does things in secret if he wants to be known openly. If You are going to do these miracles, then show Yourself to the world." For even His brothers did not believe in Him. Then Jesus said to them, "My time has not come yet, but your time is always ready. The world cannot hate you, but it hates Me because I accuse it of evil works. You go on to the feast; I will not go yet, for My time has not yet fully come." After He had said these words, He stayed for a while in Galilee.

But after His brothers were gone to the feast, He also left for the feast, though not openly. The Jews were looking for Him at the feast and they said, "Where is He?" And there was dispute among the people concerning Him, for some said, "He is a good man." And others said, "No, He deceives the people." However, no one was speaking openly of Him because they feared the Jews.

About halfway through the feast, Jesus went into the temple and He was teaching, and the Jews were marveling at His teaching. And they said, "How does this Man know all of these things without a formal education?" Jesus answered them and said, "My doctrine is not Mine, but it's from Him who sent Me. If any man will do His will, he will know the doctrine, whether it is of God or whether I speak of Myself. He who speaks of himself seeks his own glory, but He who seeks the glory of the One who sent Him is true, and there is no unrighteousness in Him. Moses gave you the law and yet none of you keep the law. Why are you plotting to kill Me?"

The people answered and said, "You have a devil. Who's plotting to kill you?" Jesus answered them, "I have done one work and you're all marveling. Moses gave you the rite of circumcision (not because it is of Moses, but of the fathers) and yet on the Sabbath day you circumcise a man. If a man is circumcised on the Sabbath day, that the law of Moses should not be broken, why are you angry with Me because I made a man completely well on the Sabbath day? Don't judge according to appearance, but judge righteous judgment."

Then some of them who were from Jerusalem said,

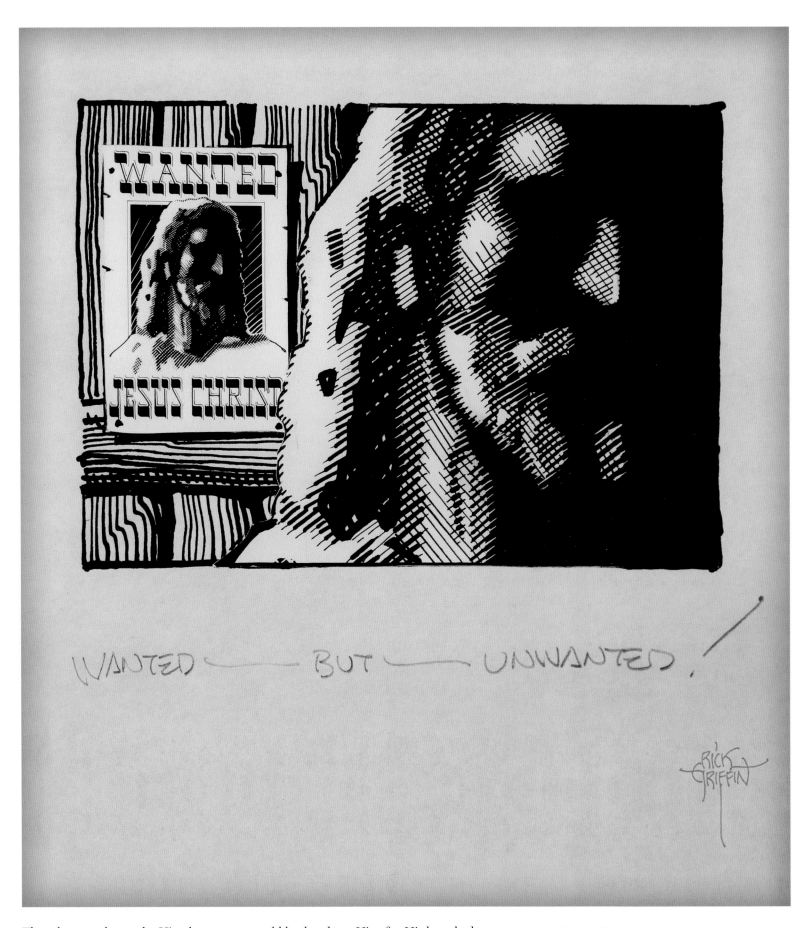

Then they sought to take Him, but no one would lay hands on Him, for His hour had not yet come. **JOHN 7:30**

"Isn't this the One whom they seek to kill? But look, He is speaking boldly and they're not saying anything to Him. Do you suppose that the rulers know that this is the Christ? However, we know this Man and where He comes from, but when the Messiah comes, no man will know where He came from." Then as Jesus was teaching in the temple, He cried, "You know Me and you know where I came from, but I am the representative of the One who sent Me. He is true and you do not know Him. I know Him, for I came from Him, and He sent Me." Then they sought to take Him, but no one would lay hands on Him, for His hour had not yet come. And

Many of the people when they heard this saying, said, "Truly this Man is the Prophet." Others said, "This is the Messiah." But some of them said, "Will the Messiah come out of Galilee? Has not the Scripture said that the Messiah comes from the seed of David and out of the town of Bethlehem where David lived?" So there was a division among the people because of Him, and some of them would have arrested Him but no man would lay hands on Him.

When the officers returned, the chief priests and the Pharisees said to them, "Why haven't you arrested

No man has ever spoken like this Man.

many of the people believed in Him and said, "When the Messiah comes, will He do any more miracles than all of these which this Man has done?"

When the Pharisees heard that the people were disputing such things concerning Him, the Pharisees and the chief priests sent officers to take Him. Then Jesus said to them, "I will be with you a little while longer, and then I am going back to Him who sent Me. You will seek Me but you will not find Me. Where I am, you cannot come." Then the Jews said among themselves, "Where is He going that we will not be able to find Him? Will He go to the Jews who have been dispersed among the Gentiles and teach the Gentiles? What kind of a saying is this, 'You will look for Me but you will not find Me, and where I am you cannot come'?"

On the last day, the great day of the feast, Jesus stood and cried, "If any man is thirsty, let him come to Me and drink. He who believes on Me, as the Scriptures have said, out of his innermost being there will gush torrents of living water." He was referring to the Spirit which those who believed on Him would receive, for the Holy Spirit was not given yet, because Jesus was not yet glorified.

Him?" The officers answered, "No man has ever spoken like this Man." The Pharisees answered them, "Are you also deceived? Have any of the rulers or the Pharisees believed in Him? Have any but the simple people who do not know the law and are cursed?" Nicodemus (the one who came to Jesus by night) said to them, "Does our law judge any man before it hears him and knows what he is doing?" They answered him, "Are you also in league with the Galilean? Search and look in the Scriptures, for out of Galilee there has never arisen a prophet." So every man went to his own house. ✝

Hope for a Harlot

INSTEAD OF CONDEMNING HER TO DEATH, JESUS FORGIVES A WOMAN OF ADULTERY † HE TELLS THE PEOPLE THAT HE, NOT THEIR RELIGIOUS SYSTEM, IS THE SPIRITUAL LIGHT • CHRIST CLAIMS TO BE THE "I AM," THE ETERNAL GOD † THE RELIGIOUS LEADERS TRY TO KILL HIM, BUT FAIL

CHAPTER EIGHT

ESUS WENT to the Mount of Olives, and early in the morning He came again to the temple, and all of the people gathered around Him. He sat down and taught them. Then the scribes and the Pharisees brought to Him a woman who was caught in adultery. When they had set her in the middle, they said to Him, "Master, this woman was taken in the very act of adultery. Moses in the law commanded us to stone her, but what do You say?" They said this in order to trap Him, for they were seeking to develop a case against Him. Jesus stooped and with His finger wrote on the ground, ignoring them. When they continued asking Him, He stood up and said to them, "Let the one who is without sin among you throw the first stone at her." Again He stooped down and wrote on the ground. When they heard this, they were convicted by their own consciences, and they left one by one, beginning with the oldest. When Jesus was left alone with the woman, He stood up and said to her, "Woman, where are your accusers? Doesn't any man condemn you?" She said, "No man, Lord." Jesus said to her, "Neither do I condemn you. Go your way and do not sin again."

Then Jesus spoke to the people saying, "I am the Light of the world. He who follows Me will not walk in darkness, but will have the light of life." The Pharisees said to Him, "Now You are witnessing of Yourself. We cannot accept this witness as true." Jesus answered them, "Though I witness of Myself, still My witness is true, for I know where I came from and where I am going. You judge by what you think you can see. I judge no man and yet if I did judge, My judgment would be true, for I am not alone, but the Father who sent Me is with Me. It is also written in your law that the testimony of two men is true. I, for one, bear witness of Myself, and the Father who sent Me bears witness of Me." Then they said to Him, "Where is Your Father?" Jesus answered, "You do not know Me nor do you know My Father. If you had known Me, you would have also known My Father." Jesus spoke these words near the treasury, as He taught in the temple. And no man laid hands on Him for His hour had not yet arrived.

Then said Jesus to them, "I am going My way, and you're going to seek Me, and you will die in your sins, for where I am going you cannot come." Then the Jews wondered if He was going to kill Himself, because He said, "Where I am going you cannot come." He said to them, "You are from beneath, and I am from above. You are of this world and I am not of this world. That is why I said to you that you will die in your sins, for if you do not believe that I AM, you will die in your sins."

"Moses in the law commanded us to stone her, but what do You say?" They said this in order to trap Him, for they were seeking to develop a case against Him. Jesus stooped and with His finger wrote on the ground, ignoring them. **JOHN 8:5-6**

Then they said to Him, "Who are You?" Jesus said, "The same One that I said to you from the beginning. I have many things to teach you and to judge you for but I will say only those things which I have heard from Him who sent Me, for He is true." They did not understand that He was speaking to them of the Father. Then Jesus said to them, "When you have lifted up the Son of Man, then you will know that I AM, and that I did nothing on My own, but only spoke the things My Father taught Me. He that sent Me is with Me; the Father has not left Me alone, for I always do those things that please Him." As He spoke these words, many believed in Him.

Father, you would love Me, for I came from God. I did not come of My own volition, but He sent Me. You do not understand what I am telling you because you do not hear My words. You are of your father, the devil, and the desires of your father, you will do. He was a murderer from the beginning, and he did not remain in the truth, because there is no truth in him. When he lies, he speaks after his own nature, for he is a liar and the father of lies. And because I tell you the truth, you do not believe Me. Which of you can point out any sin in Me? If I say the truth, why do you not believe Me? He who is of God will hear God's words; you don't hear them because you are not of God."

Let the one who is without sin among you
⟶ throw the first stone. ⟵

Then Jesus said to those Jews that did believe in Him, "If you continue in My word, then you are My disciples, and you will know the truth and the truth will make you free." The others said to Him, "We are Abraham's descendants, and we were never in bondage to any man; what do You mean 'You will be made free'?" Jesus answered them, "I tell you the truth, whoever commits sin becomes the servant of sin. The servant will not abide in the house forever, but the Son abides forever. If the Son makes you free, you will be free indeed. I know that you are Abraham's descendants, but you seek to kill Me because My words have found no place in your hearts. I am telling you what I have seen with My Father, but you do what you have seen with your father."

They answered Him, "Abraham is our father." But Jesus said to them, "If you were Abraham's children, you would do the works of Abraham. But now you seek to kill Me, a Man who has told you the truth which I have heard from God. Abraham didn't do this. You do the deeds of your father." They said to Him, "We weren't born from fornication. We have one Father, even God." Jesus said to them, "If God were your

Then the Jews answered Him and said, "Didn't we say the truth when we said that You are a Samaritan and have a devil?" Jesus answered, "I don't have a devil, but I honor My Father and you dishonor Me. I don't seek My own glory; there is One who seeks and judges. I tell you the truth: if a man keeps My saying, he will never die." Then the Jews said to Him, "Now we know that You have a devil, for Abraham is dead and so are the prophets. And You say if a man keeps Your sayings he will never taste of death. Are You greater than our father Abraham, who is dead and the prophets who are dead? Who are You trying to make Yourself?" Jesus answered, "If I honored Myself, My honor would be nothing. It is My Father who honors Me, and you say that He is your God. Yet you have not known Him. I know Him, and if I would say that I do not know Him, then I would be a liar just like you. But I know Him and I keep His word. Your father, Abraham, rejoiced to see My day, and he saw it and was glad." Then the Jews said to Him, "You're not even fifty years old; have You seen Abraham?" Jesus said to them, "I tell you the truth: before Abraham was, I AM." Then they took up stones to throw at Him, but Jesus hid Himself and went out of the temple, passing through the crowd. ✝

Sight to the Blind

JESUS, THE LIGHT OF THE WORLD, MIRACULOUSLY OPENS THE EYES OF A MAN BORN BLIND ✝ SINCE THIS HAPPENS
ON THE SABBATH DAY, THE RELIGIOUS LEADERS ARE ENRAGED

CHAPTER NINE

A**S JESUS WAS WALKING** along, He saw a man who was blind from his birth. His disciples asked Him, "Master, who sinned, this man or his parents, causing the blindness?" Jesus answered, "Neither this man nor his parents."

"In order that the works of God might be manifested in him, I must do the works of Him who sent Me while there is time. For the night is coming when no man can work. As long as I am in the world, I am the Light of the world." When He had said these things, He spat on the ground and made some clay. Then He anointed the eyes of the blind man with the clay, and He said to him, "Go wash in the pool of Siloam" (which means "Sent"). And the man went and washed, and he was able to see. When his neighbors and those who knew that he was blind saw him, they asked, "Isn't this the one who was sitting and begging?" Some said, "Yes, it is." And others said, "Well, it looks like him." He answered them, "It's me." They said to him, "How is it that you can see?" He answered, "A Man who is called Jesus made clay and anointed my eyes and told me to go wash in the pool of Siloam. When I washed I received my sight." Then they said to him, "Where is He?" He said, "I don't know."

So they took the man who was once blind to the Pharisees. It was the Sabbath day when Jesus made the clay and opened the man's eyes. When the Pharisees asked him how he had received his sight, he said, "He put clay on my eyes and I washed and I can see." Some of the Pharisees said, "This Man could not be of God because He doesn't keep the Sabbath day." Others said, "How could a man who is a sinner do such miracles?" So there was a division among them. They asked the blind man, "What do you think of the Man who opened your eyes?" The blind man answered, "He is a prophet."

But the Jews did not believe that the man was really blind and had received his sight until they called his parents. They asked them, "Is this your son, who you say was born blind? How can he now see?" His parents answered them and said, "We know that this is our son and that he was born blind, but we don't know how it is that he can now see. He's of age, ask him. He can speak for himself." His parents said this because they feared the Jews, for the Jews had already agreed that if any man confessed that Jesus was the Messiah, he would be put out of the synagogue. Therefore, the parents said, "He's of age, ask him."

So they again called the man who was blind and said to him, "Give the praise to God, for we know that this Man is a sinner." He answered and said, "I don't know whether He is a sinner or not. I do know that once I was blind, but now I can see." They said to him again, "What did He do to you? How did He open your eyes?" He answered

I must do the works of Him who sent Me while there is time.
For the night is coming when no man can work.

JOHN 9:4

them, "I told you once, but you didn't hear me. Would you hear if I told you again? Do you want to become His disciples?" And they insulted him and said, "You are His disciple, but we are Moses' disciples. We know that God spoke to Moses, but as for this Fellow, we don't know where He is from." The man said to them, "My, this is a marvelous thing that you don't know where He is from, and yet He has opened my eyes. We know that God doesn't hear sinners, but if any man worships God and

As long as I am in the world, I AM the Light of the world.

does His will, the Lord will hear him. Since the world began no one has heard that any man opened the eyes of one who was born blind. If this Man were not of God, He could do nothing." They said to him, "You were born in sin, and are you trying to teach us?" Then they threw him out.

When Jesus heard that he had been thrown out, He found the man and asked, "Do you believe in the Son of God?" He answered, "Who is He, Lord, that I might believe in Him?" Jesus said, "You have seen Him and He is talking to you." He said, "Lord, I believe." And he worshiped Him. Jesus said, "For I came into this world for judgment, so that those who are blind might see, and those who see might be made blind." Some of the Pharisees which were with Him heard these words and said to Him, "Are we blind?" Jesus said to them, "If you were blind, you would have no sin. But you say you see; therefore, your sin remains." ✝

I do know that once I was blind, but now I can see.

JOHN 9:25

No Other Way

JESUS IS THE DOOR TO GOD AND HEAVEN † HE IS THE GOOD SHEPHERD WHO GIVES HIS LIFE TO SAVE HIS SHEEP
† THE RELIGIOUS LEADERS AGAIN TRY TO KILL HIM. BUT FAIL

CHAPTER TEN

ESUS SAID, "I tell you the truth, whoever does not enter by the door into the sheepfold, but tries to climb in some other way, is a thief and a robber. The shepherd enters in by the door that the gatekeeper opens for him. His sheep hear his voice, and he calls them by name and leads them out. And he goes before his sheep and they follow him, for they know his voice. They will not follow a stranger, but will run from him, for they do not know the voice of strangers." When Jesus told this parable, those listening did not understand the things that He was saying. Then Jesus explained, "I am the Door for the sheep. Those who came before Me are thieves and robbers, and the sheep did not listen to them. I am the Door and if any man will enter in by Me, he shall be saved and shall go in and out and find pasture. The thief comes only to steal and to kill and to destroy, but I have come so they might have life and that they might have it more abundantly. I am the good Shepherd. The good Shepherd gives His life for the sheep. But one who is hired to watch the sheep which are not his own will leave the sheep and flee when he sees a wolf coming. Then the wolf will catch and scatter the sheep. One who is hired runs away because he is hired and he doesn't really care for the sheep. I am the good Shepherd, and I know My sheep and they know Me, just as the Father knows Me, and I know the Father; and I lay down My life for the sheep. I have other sheep which are not in this fold, and I must also bring them. They hear My voice and there shall be one fold and one Shepherd. For this reason My Father loves Me, because I lay down My life in order that I might take it up again. No man takes My life

---

I AM the Door and if any man will enter in by Me, he shall be saved and shall go in and out and find pasture.

I know My sheep and they know Me, just as the Father knows Me, and I know the Father. **JOHN 10:14-15**

from Me, but I lay it down of My own volition. I have power to lay it down, and I have power to take it up again. This is the commandment that My Father has given Me."

Again there was a division among the Jews because of these things. Many of them said, "He has a devil. He's insane. Why do you listen to Him?" Others said, "These are not the words of a man who has a devil. Can a devil open the eyes of the blind?"

Then the Jews picked up stones to stone Him and Jesus said, "I've shown you many good works from My Father; for which of these works are you going to stone Me?" The Jews answered Him, "It isn't for a good work that we are going to stone You, but for blasphemy, because You being a Man are continually making Yourself God." Jesus answered them, "Isn't it written in your law, 'You are gods'? If the Scripture referred to them, to whom the Word of God came as 'gods', then should you say of Him Whom the Father

I AM
the good Shepherd.
The good Shepherd gives His life for the sheep.

They were in Jerusalem during the Feast of Dedication and it was winter. And as Jesus walked in the temple in Solomon's porch, the Jews surrounded Him and said to Him, "How long will You leave us in doubt? If You're the Messiah, tell us plainly." Jesus answered, "I told you and you did not believe. The miracles that I do in My Father's name also speak to you but you don't believe because you are not My sheep, as I said to you. My sheep hear My voice and I know them and they follow Me. I give them eternal life, and they will never perish, and no man will take them out of My hand. My Father, who gave them to Me, is greater than all, and no man is able to take them out of My Father's hand. I and My Father are One."

has sanctified and sent into the world, that He blasphemes because He said, 'I am the Son of God'? If I don't do the works of My Father, then don't believe Me. But if I do, though you do not believe Me, believe the works, that you may know and believe that the Father is in Me and I am in Him."

Again they tried to take Him, but He escaped out of their hands. And He went away again, beyond Jordan to the place where John first baptized and there He stayed. And many came to Him and said, "John didn't do miracles, but all the things that John spoke of this Man are true." And many believed that He was the Messiah. ✝

Death to Life

LAZARUS DIES AND IS BURIED † BY HIS WORD, JESUS BRINGS FORTH LAZARUS FROM THE GRAVE † THE RELIGIOUS LEADERS ARE MORE DETERMINED TO KILL JESUS

CHAPTER ELEVEN

HERE WAS A MAN named Lazarus who lived in Bethany with his sisters, Mary and Martha. (This was the same Mary who anointed the Lord with ointment and wiped His feet with her hair.) When Lazarus became ill, the sisters sent a message to Jesus saying, "Lord, the one You love is sick." When Jesus heard it, He said to His disciples, "This sickness is not fatal, but is for the glory of God, that the Son of God might be glorified through it."

Jesus loved Martha, Mary and Lazarus. But when He heard that Lazarus was sick, He stayed for two days in the same place where He was. Then He said to His disciples, "Let's go to Judea." His disciples asked Him, "Master, lately the Jews have tried to stone You. Are You going to go there again?" Jesus answered, "Are there not twelve hours of daylight? If any man walks in the daytime he will not stumble, because he sees the light of the world. But if a man walks at night, he stumbles because he has no light in himself." After He had said these things, He said to them, "Our friend Lazarus sleeps, but I'm going to awaken him." Then

Jesus said to her,
He that believes in Me, though he died,
yet he will live. And whoever lives
and believes in Me shall never die.
Do you believe this?

the disciples said, "Lord, if he is sleeping he should be getting better." However, Jesus was referring to his death, but they thought He was saying that Lazarus was resting. Then Jesus said to them plainly, "Lazarus is dead, and I am glad for you that I was not there so that you might believe. However, let us go to him." Then Thomas, who was called "the Twin," said to his fellow disciples, "Let's also go and die with Him."

When she had said this, she returned and said to Mary, her sister, "The Master has come and He wants to see you." As soon as Mary heard this, she arose quickly and went to Him. (Jesus had not yet arrived in the town, but was still in the place where Martha had met Him.) When the Jews who were comforting Mary saw her arise quickly and leave the house, they followed saying, "She's probably going to the grave to weep there." When Mary came to Jesus, she fell down at His feet

When Jesus arrived, He found that Lazarus had already been buried in the grave for four days. Bethany was near Jerusalem (about two-thirds of a mile away), and many of the Jews came to Martha and Mary to comfort them about their brother's death. Martha went out to meet Jesus as soon as she heard that He was coming, but Mary sat in the house. Martha said to Jesus, "Lord, if You only would have been here, my brother would not have died. But I know that even now, whatever You would ask God, God would give to You." Jesus said to her, "Your brother will live again." Martha said, "I know that he will live again at the resurrection in the last day." Jesus said to her, "He that believes in Me, though he died, yet he will live. And whoever lives and believes in Me shall never die. Do you believe this?" She said to Him, "Yes, Lord, I believe that You are the Christ, the Son of God, who they prophesied would come into the world."

and said to Him, "Lord, if You would have been here my brother would not have died." When Jesus saw her weeping and the weeping of the Jews that came with her, He was grieved in His spirit and was burdened. He said, "Where did you bury him?" They said to Him, "Lord, come and see." Jesus wept. When the Jews saw Jesus weeping, they said, "Look how much He loved him." Some of them said, "Do you suppose it's possible that this Man who opened the eyes of the blind could have prevented this man's death?"

As Jesus came to the grave, He was still grieving inwardly. The tomb was a cave with a stone over the door. Jesus said, "Take away the stone." Martha said to Him, "Lord, by this time there will be a bad odor, for he has been dead for four days." Jesus said to her, "Didn't I tell you that if you would believe, you would see the glory of God?" When they took away the stone from the place where Lazarus was buried, Jesus lifted up His eyes to heaven and said, "Father, I thank You that You have heard Me. I know that You always hear Me, but I say this for the sake of those who are listening so in hearing this they will believe that You have sent Me." When He had said this, He cried with a loud voice, "Lazarus, come out!" And Lazarus came out with his hands and feet bound with grave clothes, and his face wrapped with a napkin. Jesus said to them, "Untie him and let him go."

Many of the Jews who came with Mary saw the things which Jesus did and believed in Him. But others went to the Pharisees and told them what Jesus had done. Then the chief priests and the Pharisees gathered together in a council and said, "What shall we do, for this Man is doing many miracles? If we do not stop Him, everyone will believe in Him, and the Romans will come and take away our place of position and possibly our nation." Caiaphas, who was the high priest that year, said to them, "You don't understand these things.

Don't you realize that it's necessary that one Man should die for the people so that the whole nation will not be destroyed?" This he was speaking, not of himself, but since he was the high priest he was prophesying that Jesus should die, not just for that nation but for the world. From that day on, the Jewish leaders planned how to put Jesus to death.

At this time Jesus did not walk openly among the Jews, but went from there into an area near the wilderness, to a city that was called Ephraim. There He stayed with His disciples.

The time of the Jewish Passover Feast was near and many were coming from the country to Jerusalem to purify themselves before the Passover. They looked for Jesus and talked among themselves as they stood in the temple, speculating about whether He would come to the feast. Both the chief priests and the Pharisees had commanded that if any man knew where Jesus was, he should reveal it so that they might arrest Him. ✝

She said to Him, Yes, Lord, *I believe that You are the Christ,* the Son of God, who they prophesied would come into the world.

The Whole World is Going After Him

MARY, THE SISTER OF LAZARUS, ANOINTS CHRIST WITH OIL AND WIPES HIS FEET WITH HER HAIR † KEY PROPHECIES ARE FULFILLED AS JESUS ENTERS JERUSALEM
ON A DONKEY AND IS HAILED BY THE PEOPLE † THE VOICE OF GOD SPEAKS FROM HEAVEN

CHAPTER TWELVE

IX DAYS BEFORE THE PASSOVER Jesus went to Bethany, where Lazarus had been raised from the dead. They had a dinner for Him, and Martha was serving and Lazarus was one of those sitting at the table with Him. Then Mary took a pound of spikenard ointment, which was very expensive, and she poured it on the feet of Jesus and wiped His feet with her hair. As she did this the house was filled with a glorious aroma. Then one of the disciples, whose name was Judas Iscariot (the one who betrayed Him), said, "Why didn't you sell this perfume for $3,000 so we could have the money to give to the poor?" He did not say this because he cared for the poor, but because he was a thief, and he had charge of their common purse and was stealing from it. Then Jesus said to Him, "Let her alone; she has anointed Me for the day of My burying. For you always will have the poor with you, but you will not always have Me."

Many of the Jews knew that Jesus was there and they did not come just to see Him, but they were also curious to see Lazarus, who had been raised from the dead. So the chief priests were consulting together concerning the possibility of killing Lazarus also, because of the fact that many Jews were believing in Jesus through his resurrection from the dead.

The next day, many people who had come to the feast heard that Jesus was coming to Jerusalem and they took branches from palm trees and they went out to meet Him and they cried, "Hosanna!" or "Save now! Blessed is the King of Israel, who comes in the name of the Lord!" Jesus rode a young donkey, fulfilling what was written by the prophets, "Fear not, daughter of Zion, for your King is coming, and He is sitting on a donkey." The disciples did not understand these things at first, but later when Jesus was resurrected, they remembered all of the prophecies that were written of Him, and how they had seen them fulfilled.

The people who were with Jesus when He raised Lazarus from the dead and called him out of the grave were telling and confirming the story. So the people went out to meet Him because they had heard of this marvelous miracle. The Pharisees said in their own gatherings, "Can't you see how we're not prevailing? Look how the whole world is going after Him."

There were some men from Greece who had come to worship at the feast, and they went to Philip, who was from Bethsaida of Galilee, and they said to Philip, "Sir, we would like to see Jesus." Philip told Andrew, and together they told Jesus. Jesus said, "The hour has come for the Son of Man to be glorified. I tell you the

Jesus rode a young donkey, fulfilling what was written by the prophets, "Fear not, daughter of Zion, for your King is coming, and He is sitting on a donkey." **JOHN 12:14-15**

truth, that unless a grain of wheat falls into the ground and dies, it remains just a single grain. But if it dies, it will produce more grain. He who loves his life shall lose it, but he who disdains the life of this world shall have eternal life. If any man desires to serve Me, he must follow Me, for wherever I am, My servants will be there too. If any man serves Me, My Father will honor him. Now, My mind is troubled. What shall I say: 'Father, deliver Me from this hour'? And yet I came into the world for this hour. Father, glorify Your name."

After Jesus had said these things, He departed and hid Himself from them. Even though He had done so many miracles before them, they still did not believe in Him, in order that the saying of Isaiah the prophet might be fulfilled when he declared, "Lord, who has believed our report, and who will accept Your miracles as proof?" Besides, they could not believe, because Isaiah also said, "He has blinded their eyes and hardened their hearts, so that they cannot see with their eyes, nor understand with their hearts, and be converted and be healed." Isaiah declared these things when he saw a vision of

Hosanna!
or Save now!
Blessed is the King of Israel,
who comes in the name of the Lord!

Then a voice from heaven said, "I have glorified My name, and I will glorify it again." Some people who were standing by and heard the voice thought that it had thundered, but others said an angel spoke to Him. Jesus said, "This voice did not come for My sake, but for yours. The time has come for the judgment of this world. Now the prince of this world, Satan, will be cast out, and when I am lifted up from the earth, I will draw all men to Me." By His reference to being lifted up He was indicating He was to die by crucifixion. The people answered Him, "We have heard that the law says that the Messiah will live forever. How is it that You are saying that the Son of Man must be lifted up? Who is this Son of Man?" Then Jesus said to them, "A little longer the Light will be with you. Walk while you have the Light, for the darkness is coming upon you. For he who walks in darkness does not know where he is going. While you have the Light, believe in the Light, so that you will be the children of Light."

Jesus' glory and prophesied of Him. Nevertheless, among the chief rulers there were many who believed in Him, but because of the Pharisees they did not openly confess Him, for they did not want to be put out of the synagogue, because they loved the praise of men more than the praise of God.

Jesus cried and said, "He who believes in Me, believes not in Me but in Him who sent Me. And he who sees Me sees Him who sent Me. I have come as a light into the world, whoever believes in Me will not live in darkness. If any man hears My words and does not believe, I do not judge him, for I did not come to judge the world, but to save the world. He who rejects Me and does not receive My words has one who judges him; the word which I have spoken will be his judge in the last day. For I have not spoken My own feelings, but the Father who sent Me has given Me commandments as to what I should say. I know that to keep His commandment means everlasting life, so whatever I have spoken has been what the Father has told Me to speak." ✝

The Upper Room

JESUS INSTRUCTS HIS DISCIPLES DURING THE PASSOVER MEAL ON THE EVE OF HIS ARREST AND CRUCIFIXION
✝ JUDAS DECIDES TO TURN HIM OVER TO THE RELIGIOUS AUTHORITIES ✝ JESUS WASHES THE FEET OF HIS DISCIPLES AND PREDICTS PETER'S DENIAL

CHAPTER THIRTEEN

N THE NIGHT of the Feast of the Passover, Jesus knew that His hour had come and that He would leave this world and go back to the Father. He loved His disciples to the utmost. After the supper, the devil put into the heart of Judas Iscariot, Simon's son, the desire to betray Jesus. Jesus knew that the Father had placed everything into His hands and that He had come from God and was going to God. So He rose from the supper and laid aside His garments and clothed Himself as a servant and took a towel. He then poured water into a basin and began to wash the disciples' feet and to wipe them with the towel. When He came to Simon Peter, Peter said to Him, "Lord, why are You going to wash my feet?" Jesus said, "What I am doing you do not know now, but you will know later on." Peter said to Him, "You will never wash my feet." Jesus answered, "If I do not wash you, then you have no partnership with Me." Simon Peter replied, "Lord, then don't just wash my feet, but my hands and my head." Jesus said, "I only need to wash your feet and you will be completely clean, and all of you are clean, but one." For He knew who would betray Him, that is why He said, "You are all clean but one."

After He had washed their feet and put on His own garments, He sat down with them again and said to them, "Do you know what I have done to you? You call Me Master and Lord, and that is correct, for I am. Now if I am your Lord and Master, and I have washed your feet, you also ought to wash one another's feet. For I have given you an example, that you should do as I have done to you. I tell you the truth: the servant is not greater than the one who sent him. If you know these things, you will be happy if you do them. However, I do not speak to all of you, for I know whom I have chosen. The Scripture will be fulfilled: 'He who eats bread with Me has lifted up his hand against Me.' I have told you before it happens so that after it has happened, you'll believe that I AM. I tell you the truth: he who receives whoever I have sent, receives Me. He who receives Me, receives the One who sent Me."

When Jesus had said these things, He was heavy in His spirit, and He said, "I tell you the truth: one of you will betray Me." Then the disciples looked at one another, wondering which one He was referring to. Leaning on Jesus was one of the disciples who was loved by Jesus, and Simon Peter signaled to him to ask which one Jesus was talking about. So the one lying against Jesus said to Him, "Lord, who is it?" Jesus answered, "The one I shall give the bread to after I have dipped it." When He had dipped the bread, He gave it to Judas Iscariot, the son of Simon. After the bread was given, Satan entered

On the night of the Feast of Passover, Jesus knew that His hour had come
and that He would leave this world and go back to the Father.
He loved His disciples to the utmost.

JOHN 13:1

into him. Then Jesus said to him, "What you do, do quickly." No man at the table knew exactly what Jesus had said to him, for some of them thought that because Judas held the purse, that Jesus intended for him to buy certain things they would need for the feast, or that he should go out and give something to the poor. After Judas received the bread, he went immediately out

you a new commandment, that you love one another. As I have loved you, so are you to love one another. By this all men will know that you are My disciples, if you love one another." Simon Peter said to Him, "Lord, where are You going?" Jesus answered him, "Where I am going you cannot follow Me now, but you will follow Me later." Peter said to Him, "Lord, why can't I follow You now?

As I have loved you, so are you to love one another.

By this all men will know that you are My disciples, if you love one another.

into the darkness of the night. And when he was gone, Jesus said, "Now the Son of Man is glorified, and God is glorified in Him. God will also glorify Himself. Little children, I will be with you a little while longer and then you will seek Me, and even as I said to the Jews, I say to you, 'Where I am going you cannot come.' I give

I will lay down my life for You." Jesus answered him, "Will you lay down your life for Me? I tell you the truth: before the rooster crows, you will have denied Me three times." ✝

The Way

JESUS CONTINUES TO EXPLAIN SPIRITUAL THINGS TO HIS DISCIPLES † HE IS THE WAY, THE TRUTH, AND THE LIFE
† HE PROMISES TO SEND THEM THE HOLY SPIRIT, THE COMFORTER

CHAPTER FOURTEEN

ET NOT your heart be troubled. You believe in God, believe also in Me. In My Father's house there are many abiding places. If this weren't true, I would have told you. I'm going to prepare a place for you, and if I go and prepare a place for you, I will come again and get you so that you might be with Me. Where I am going you know, and the way you know." Thomas said to Him, "Lord, we don't know where You are going, and how can we know the way?" Jesus said, "I am the way, the truth and the life. No man comes to the Father unless he comes through Me. If you have known Me, you should have known My Father also, and from now on you do know Him and have seen Him."

Philip said to Him, "Lord, if You will only show us the Father, we will be satisfied." Jesus said to him, "Have I been with you this long and yet have you not known Me, Philip? He who has seen Me has seen the Father. How is it that you say, 'Show us the Father'? Do you not believe that I am in the Father and the Father in Me? The words that I am speaking to you I do not speak on My own, they are from the Father who dwells in Me. He is the One doing the miracles through Me. Believe Me, that I am in the Father and the Father is in Me, or else believe Me for the miracles that I do."

"I tell you the truth: he who believes in Me, the miracles that I do, will he do also, and even greater miracles will he do because I am going to My Father. Whatever you will ask in My name, I will do it, that the Father may be

If I go and prepare a place for you,

I will come again

and get you so that you might be with Me.

Jesus said,

I AM
THE WAY,
the Truth and the Life.
No man comes to the Father
unless he comes
through Me.

glorified in the Son. If you ask anything in My name, I will do it."

"If you love Me, keep My commandments. I will pray to the Father that He will send another Comforter to you, and He will stay with you forever. He is the Spirit of truth whom the world cannot receive because it cannot see Him, and it doesn't know Him. But you know Him, for He dwells with you and He shall be in you."

which you hear are not really Mine; they are the Father's who sent Me."

"These things I have told you while I am still with you, but the Comforter, who is the Holy Spirit, whom the Father will send in My name, will teach you all things and bring everything to your memory that I have said to you. Peace I leave with you, not the pseudo peace of the world, but My peace. Don't be worried and don't

I will not leave you without help.
I will come to you. In just a little while
the world will not see Me anymore,
but you will see Me,

and because *I live, you will live also.*

In that day you will know that I am in My Father
and you are in Me, and I am in you.

"I will not leave you without help. I will come to you. In just a little while the world will not see Me anymore, but you will see Me, and because I live, you will live also. In that day you will know that I am in My Father, and you are in Me, and I am in you. Whoever has My commandments and keeps them, loves Me. Those who love Me shall be loved by My Father and I will love them, and We will manifest Ourselves to them." Judas (not Judas Iscariot) said to Him, "Lord, how is it that You will manifest Yourself to us and not to the world?" Jesus answered, "If a man loves Me, he will keep the things I have said and My Father will love him, and We will make Our home with him. The one who does not keep My sayings does not love Me, and these sayings

be afraid. You have heard Me say to you that I am going away and am coming again. If you loved Me, you would rejoice because I said that I was going to My Father, for My Father is greater than I. I have told you these things before they happen so that when they do occur, you will believe. From now on, I will not have a chance to talk much with you, for the prince of this world is coming. He does not have any power over Me, but that the world will know that I love the Father, I will do what the Father has commanded Me. Arise, and let's be going." ✝

The True Vine

JESUS AND THE DISCIPLES WALK TO THE GARDEN OF GETHSEMANE † HE TELLS THEM THAT HE IS THE TRUE VINE, THE SOURCE OF ALL SPIRITUAL LIFE † HE FOREWARNS THEM ABOUT PERSECUTION FROM THE WORLD

CHAPTER FIFTEEN

 AM THE TRUE VINE and My Father is the gardener. Every branch in Me that does not bear fruit He takes away. Every branch that does bear fruit He cleanses and washes, that it might produce more fruit. Now you are clean through the word which I have spoken to you. Live in Me and I will live in you. The branch cannot bear fruit by itself unless it lives in the vine; neither can you unless you live in Me. I am the vine and you are the branches. He who lives in Me and I in him will produce much fruit, for without Me you can do nothing. If a man does not live in Me, he is cast forth as a branch, and he withers, and men gather the withered branches and throw them into the fire and they are burned. If you live in Me and My words live in you, you will ask what you desire and it will be done for you. My Father is glorified when you bear much fruit, thus showing true discipleship. As the Father has loved Me, so have I loved you. Continue in My love. If you keep My commandments, then you live in My love, even as I have kept My Father's commandments and live in His love. I have spoken to you these things that My joy might remain in you and that your joy might be full."

"This is My commandment, that you love one another as I have loved you. There is no greater love than this: that a man gives his life for his friends. You are My friends if you do what I command you. From now on, I do not

I AM the Vine
and you are the branches. He who lives
in Me and I in him will produce much fruit,
for without Me you can do nothing.

Now you are clean through the word which I have spoken to you.
Live in Me and I will live in you. The branch cannot bear fruit by itself
unless it lives in the vine, neither can you unless you live in Me.

JOHN 15:3-4

call you servants, for the servant does not know what his lord is doing, but I call you friends for I have told you the things that I have heard from My Father. You did not choose Me, but I chose you and ordained you to go and produce lasting fruit. Whatever you ask the Father in My name, He will give to you."

"I command you to love one another. If the world hates you, remember that it hated Me before it hated you. If you were of this world, the world would love you, but the reason the world hates you is because I chose you out of the world. Now remember the words that I said to you, 'The servant is not greater than his lord.' If they have persecuted Me, they will also persecute you. If they have not kept My sayings, they will not keep yours. They will do these things to you because of Me and because they don't know Him who sent Me. Had I not come and spoken to them, they would not have been conscious of their sin, but now they have no covering for their sin. He who hates Me hates My Father also. If I had not done among them the miracles which no other man has done, then they would not have been considered guilty of sin. But now they have both seen the miracles and hated My Father and Me. This has come to pass, that the word might be fulfilled which was written in their law, 'They hated Me without a cause.' I will send the Comforter to you, the Spirit of truth who comes from the Father, and He will testify of Me. You also will tell others about Me because you have been with Me from the beginning." ✝

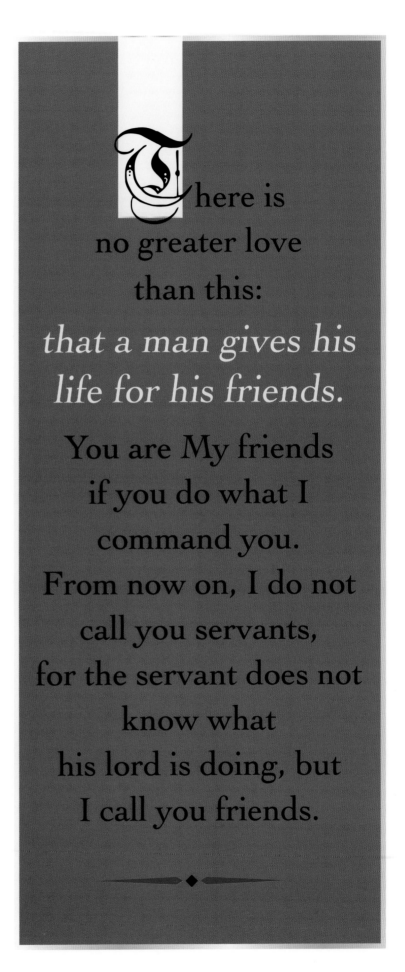

There is
no greater love
than this:
that a man gives his
life for his friends.

You are My friends
if you do what I
command you.
From now on, I do not
call you servants,
for the servant does not
know what
his lord is doing, but
I call you friends.

The Coming Comforter

JESUS WARNS THAT SOME OF THE DISCIPLES WILL BE MARTYRED † HE EXPLAINS THE WORK OF THE HOLY SPIRIT
AND EXPOUNDS ON HIS DEPARTURE FROM THE EARTH [WORLD]

CHAPTER SIXTEEN

HAVE TOLD YOU these things so that you will not be offended, for they shall put you out of the synagogues. The time will even come that whoever kills you will think that he is doing God a service, and they will do these things to you because they have not known the Father nor Me. But I've told you these things so that when the time comes you might remember that I forewarned you about them."

"I did not tell you these things at the beginning because I was still with you, but now I am going back to Him who sent Me. Yet none of you ask Me, 'Where are You going?' Because I have said these things to you, your hearts have been filled with sorrow. Nevertheless, I tell you the truth: it is necessary for you that I go away, for if I do not go away, the Comforter will not come to you. But if I depart, I will send Him to you. When He comes, He will convict the world of sin and of righteousness and of judgment. The sin is that they did not believe in Me. My ascending to the Father is a witness to the world of the standard of righteousness He will accept. The judgment has come upon the prince of this world."

"I have many things to tell you, but you can't bear them at the present time. However, when the Spirit of truth has come, He will guide you into all truth, for He will not speak of Himself, but whatever He shall hear, those are the things that He will speak. He will show you the things that are going to take place. He will glorify Me, for He shall receive from Me and tell it to you. I am all that the Father is, that is why I said that the Holy

When He comes,
He will convict the world of sin and of righteousness and of judgment.

I have told these things to you
so that you will have peace.
In this world you will
have trouble and sadness.
But be cheerful, for

I HAVE OVERCOME
THE WORLD.

◆

Spirit will reveal Me to you. In a little while you will not see Me and then a little while later you will see Me, because I'm going to the Father."

Then some of the disciples questioned among themselves, "What is He talking about, 'A little while and you will not see Me, and a little while later you will see Me, because I'm going to My Father'?" They said, "What is He talking about, a little while? We don't know what He is trying to tell us." Jesus knew that they desired to ask Him these questions so He said to them, "Are you questioning among yourselves about what I said, 'In a little while you will not see Me, and

not asked in My name. Please ask, and you will receive, and your joy will be full."

"I have spoken these things to you in proverbs, but the time is coming when I will no longer speak to you in proverbs, but I shall speak plainly the things of the Father. In that day you will ask in My name and I will not have to ask the Father for you, for the Father Himself loves you because you've loved Me and have believed that I have come from God. I came from the Father into the world and now I am leaving the world and going to the Father."

When the Spirit of truth has come He will guide you into all truth, for He will not speak of Himself, but whatever He shall hear, those are the things that He will speak. He will show you the things that are going to take place.

---

then a little while later you will see Me'? I tell you the truth, that you will weep and be sad, but the world will be rejoicing. You will be very sorrowful, but your sorrow will be turned into joy. A woman when she is in labor has sorrow because her time has come, but as soon as the child is delivered, she does not remember the anguish because she has such joy that her child has been born. Now you have sorrow, but when I see you again your hearts will rejoice, and no man will be able to take that joy from you. In that day you will not need to ask Me for anything, for the Father will give to you whatever you ask for in My name. Before now you have

His disciples said to Him, "Now You are speaking to us plainly and not in proverbs. Now we are sure that You know everything and You do not need men to tell You anything. By this we believe that You did come from God." Jesus said, "Do you now believe? The hour is coming and is even here when you will be scattered, every man by himself, and you will leave Me alone, yet I am never alone because the Father is with Me. I have told these things to you so that you will have peace. In this world you will have trouble and sadness. But be cheerful, for I have overcome the world." ✝

Our Intercessor

JESUS PRAYS THAT GOD KEEPS HIS PRESENT AND FUTURE DISCIPLES FROM STRAYING
AND SETS THEM APART THROUGH THE TRUTH, AND THAT THEY ALL MAY BE ONE.

CHAPTER SEVENTEEN

FTER JESUS SAID these words, He lifted up His eyes to heaven and said, "Father, the time has come. Glorify Your Son, so that Your Son may also glorify You. For You have given Him power over all men and women to give eternal life to as many as You have given Him. This is the way to eternal life, that they know You, the only true God, and Jesus Christ whom You sent. I have glorified

"I have spoken of You to these men You gave Me out of the world. They were Yours and You gave them to Me, and they have obeyed You. They have known that all of the things You have given to Me are from You. I have given them the words which You gave Me, and they have received them, and they know for sure that I came from You and they have believed that You sent Me. I pray for them. I do not pray for the world, but for these whom You have given Me, for they are Yours. I am Yours and You are Mine, and I rejoice in them.

This is the way to eternal life, that they know You, the only true God, and Jesus Christ whom You sent.

You on the earth and I have finished the work which You gave Me to do. Now Father, glorify Me with Your own presence and with the glory that I had with You before the world ever was."

Now I am leaving the world, but they are staying in the world. I will be leaving them to come to You. Holy Father, keep those whom You have given Me in the power of Your name so they will be one, as We are one.

After Jesus said these words, He lifted up His eyes to heaven and said,
"Father, the time has come. Glorify Your Son, so that Your Son may also glorify You."

JOHN 17:1

While I was with them in the world, I kept them in Your name. I have kept those whom You gave to Me and none of them is lost, except the son of perdition, for the Scripture must be fulfilled. Now I am coming to You, and I spoke these things to them that they will be full of My joy. I have given them Your word, and the world has hated them because they are not of the world, even as I am not of the world. I do not pray that You would take them out of the world, but that You would keep them from the power of Satan. They are not of the world, even as I am not of the world. Now set them apart through Your truth, for Your word is truth. As You have sent Me into the world, I have also sent them into the world. And for their sakes I set Myself apart, so that they also would be set apart through the truth."

"I do not pray for just these, but for those also who will believe in Me through their witness, that they may all be one, as You, Father, are in Me, and I am in You. May they also be one in Us, so the world will believe that You sent Me. The glory which You gave to Me I have given to them, so they will be one, even as We are one. I in them, and You in Me, so that they will be made perfect in One, and so the world will know that You have sent Me and have loved them as You loved Me. Father, I desire that these whom You have given to Me might be with Me and see My glory which You have given to Me. For You loved Me before the world ever existed. Oh righteous Father, the world does not know You, but I have known You and these whom You have sent to Me know You. I have revealed You to them and I will continue to reveal You so that Your love for Me will be in them, as I am in them." ✝

I do not pray for just these, but for those also who will believe in Me through their witness, that they may all be one, as You, Father, are in Me, and I am in You.

Midnight Arrest

JESUS IS ARRESTED IN THE GARDEN OF GETHSEMANE BY THE RELIGIOUS AUTHORITIES AND TAKEN TO THE HIGH PRIEST
✝ PETER AND JOHN FOLLOW ✝ PETER DENIES THAT HE IS CHRIST'S DISCIPLE ✝ THE JEWS TAKE JESUS TO PILATE, THE CIVIL AUTHORITY

CHAPTER EIGHTEEN

HEN JESUS had spoken these words, He went out with His disciples over the brook Kidron and to the garden. Judas, who betrayed Him, knew the place where Jesus often went with His disciples. Judas was given a band of men and officers from the chief priests and the Pharisees, and he came into the garden with lanterns, torches and weapons. Jesus, knowing all things that were going to happen to Him, went forward and said to them, "Who are you looking for?" They answered Him, "Jesus of Nazareth." Jesus said to them, "I AM." And as soon as He had said to them, "I AM," they fell backward on the ground. Then He asked them again, "Who are you looking for?" They said, "Jesus of Nazareth." Jesus answered, "I have told you that I AM. If you are looking for Me, let these others go." He said this in order that His saying might be fulfilled when He said, "I did not lose one of those You gave to Me." Then Simon Peter drew his sword and cut off the right ear of Malchus, the servant of the high priest. Jesus said to Peter, "Put your sword back into the sheath. Shall I not drink the cup which the Father has given Me?"

Then the band of men and the captain and the officers of the Jews took Jesus and bound Him and led Him away to Annas first, for he was the father-in-law of Caiaphas, who was the high priest that year. Caiaphas was the one who counseled the Jews that it was necessary that one Man should die for all the people.

Simon Peter and another disciple followed Jesus. Peter stood outside at the door while the other disciple, knowing the high priest, went along with Jesus into the palace. Then the disciple who knew the high priest went out and spoke to the girl who was watching the door and brought Peter in. The young girl that kept the door said to Peter, "Are you also one of Jesus' disciples?" He said, "I am not." The servants and the officers had made a fire of coals, for it was cold, and they were warming themselves, and Peter stood with them and warmed himself.

The high priest then asked Jesus about His disciples and about His doctrine. Jesus answered him, "I spoke openly to the world; I taught often in the synagogues and in the temple where the Jews always go, and I have said nothing in secret, so why do you ask Me? Ask those who heard Me what I have said to them. They know what I have said." When Jesus said this, one of

Jesus said to them, "I AM." And as soon as He had said to them, "I AM," they fell backward on the ground. **JOHN 18:6**

you in the garden with Him?" Peter again denied and immediately the rooster crowed.

Then they led Jesus from Caiaphas to the hall of judgment and it was still early in the morning. The Jews would not go into the judgment hall because they did not want to be defiled, for they wanted to eat the Passover meal. So Pilate went out to them and asked, "What accusation do you make against this Man?" They answered him, "If He were not a criminal, we would not have brought Him to you." Then Pilate said to them, "Take Him and judge Him according to your own law." The Jews said to him, "It is unlawful for us to put any man to death." This meant the saying of Jesus would be fulfilled, when He had predicted that crucifixion was

the officers who stood by struck Jesus with the palm of his hand, saying, "Is that the way You answer the high priest?" Jesus said to him, "If I have spoken evil, prove it. If I have spoken the truth, why do you hit Me?" Annas had bound Him and sent Him to Caiaphas, the high priest.

As Simon Peter was warming himself by the fire, the others with him said to him, "Aren't you one of His disciples?" He denied it saying, "No." One of the servants of the high priest, who was a relative of the servant whose ear Peter cut off, said, "Didn't I see

That's right, I am a King.

For this reason
I was born
and for this purpose
I came into the world,
that I should
bring the truth.
Everyone that
desires the truth
listens to My voice.

One of the servants of the high priest, who was a relative of the servant whose ear Peter cut off, said, "Didn't I see you in the garden with Him?" Peter again denied and immediately the rooster crowed. **JOHN 18:26-27**

how He would die. Then Pilate went into the judgment hall again and called Jesus. He asked Him, "Are You the King of the Jews?" Jesus answered him, "Do you ask this question yourself, or did others tell you to ask Me?" Pilate said, "Am I a Jew? Your own nation and the chief priests delivered You to me. What have You done?" Jesus answered him, "My kingdom is not of this world. If My kingdom were of this world, then My servants would fight to keep Me from being delivered to the Jews. But My kingdom is not here." Pilate then said to Him, "Are You a King?" Jesus answered, "That's right, I am a King. For this reason I was born and for this purpose I came into the world, that I should bring the truth. Everyone that desires the truth listens to My voice." Pilate said to Him, "What is truth?" When he had said this, he went out again to the Jews and said to them, "I find no fault in this Man. But you have a custom that I should release a prisoner at the Passover. Do you want me to release the King of the Jews?" Then they all cried together, "Not this Man, but Barabbas." Barabbas was a robber. ✝

My kingdom
is not of this world.

If My kingdom
were of this world,
then My servants
would fight
to keep Me
from being delivered
to the Jews.
But My kingdom
is not here.

The Killing of God

JESUS IS SCOURGED. THE JEWS DEMAND HIS CRUCIFIXION ✝ PILATE SENTENCES JESUS TO DEATH ✝ FROM THE CROSS JESUS GIVES HIS MOTHER
INTO JOHN'S CARE, CRIES IN THIRST, AND FINALLY GIVES UP HIS SPIRIT ✝ NICODEMUS AND JOSEPH OF ARIMATHEA TAKE HIS BODY AND BURY IT IN A NEW TOMB

CHAPTER NINETEEN

HEN PILATE had Jesus whipped and the soldiers made a crown of thorns which they put on His head. They put a purple robe on Him and said, "Hail, King of the Jews." And they struck Him with their hands. Pilate again went out and said to the Jews, "I'm bringing Him out to you, so you will know that I find no fault in Him." Then Jesus came out wearing the crown of thorns and the purple robe, and Pilate said to them, "Behold the Man." When the chief priests and the officers saw Him, they cried out, "Crucify! Crucify!" Pilate said to them, "Would you crucify Him? I find no fault in Him." The Jews answered him, "We have a law and by our law He ought to die because He was continually making Himself the Son of God." When Pilate heard this, he was even more frightened, and he went again into the judgment hall and said to Jesus, "Where did You come from?" But Jesus would not answer him. Then Pilate asked, "Won't You answer me? Don't You know that I have the power to crucify You or to release You?" Jesus answered, "You could have no power at all against Me, unless it was given to you from above. Therefore the ones that delivered Me to you have the greater sin."

From that time Pilate tried to release Him, but the Jews cried out, "If you let this Man go, you are not Caesar's friend, for whoever makes himself a king is against Caesar." When Pilate heard this, he brought Jesus out and he sat down in the judgment seat in a place that is called "The Pavement" (in Hebrew, *Gabbatha*). It was time for the preparation of the Passover, about the sixth hour, when Pilate said to the Jews, "Behold your King!" But they cried out, "Away with Him, away with Him! Crucify Him!" Pilate said to them, "Shall I crucify your King?" The chief priest answered, "We have no king but Caesar." Pilate then delivered Him to be crucified.

So they took Jesus and led Him away. Jesus, carrying the cross, went to a place called "The Skull," which in Hebrew is called *Golgotha*. There they crucified Him with two others, one on either side, with Jesus in the middle. Pilate wrote a title and put it on the cross and it said, "JESUS OF NAZARETH, THE KING OF THE JEWS." Many of the Jews read this title, for the place where Jesus was crucified was near the city and it was written in Hebrew, Greek and Latin. Then the chief priest of the Jews said to Pilate, "Don't write 'The King of the Jews,' but write 'He said, I am the King of the Jews.'" Pilate said, "What I have written, I have written."

There they crucified Him with two others, one on either side, with Jesus in the middle. **JOHN 19:18**

Then the soldiers, when they had crucified Jesus, took His garments and divided them among the four of them, and each soldier received a part. They also took His coat which was seamless, for it was woven from the top all the way through. They said to each other, "Let's not tear this, but let's throw dice for it to find out whose it will be." This fulfilled the Scripture which said, "They parted My clothing among them, and for My robe they cast lots." These are the things that the soldiers did.

these things were prophesied in the Scriptures, which said, "Not a bone of Him shall be broken," and "They shall look on Him whom they pierced."

After this, Joseph of Arimathea, who was a secret disciple of Jesus because he feared the Jews, begged Pilate to allow him to take the body of Jesus away. Pilate gave him permission, and he came and took the body of Jesus. Nicodemus, who came at night to Jesus at the beginning

When Jesus had tasted the vinegar, He cried,
— It is finished. —
And He bowed His head and dismissed His Spirit.

There stood by the cross of Jesus His mother, and His mother's sister, and Mary the wife of Cleophas, and Mary Magdalene. When Jesus saw His mother standing by the disciple whom He loved, He said to her, "Woman, behold your son," and He said to the disciple, "Behold your mother." From that hour the disciple took her into his own home.

After this, Jesus knew that everything was accomplished and the Scriptures were fulfilled, and He said, "I'm thirsty." There was a jar full of vinegar there, and they filled a sponge with vinegar and put it on a hyssop branch and touched it to His mouth. When Jesus had tasted the vinegar, He cried, "It is finished." And He bowed His head and dismissed His Spirit.

The Jews, because it was the day of preparation and they did not want the bodies to remain on the cross on the Sabbath day (for it was the high day of the feast), went to Pilate and asked that the prisoners' legs be broken (to hasten death) so they could be taken away. So the soldiers broke the legs of the two who were crucified with Jesus, but seeing that Jesus was already dead, they did not break His legs. However, one of the soldiers pierced Jesus' side with his spear and blood and water came out. When the disciple saw it, he wrote it down and relayed this truth to you so that you might believe. For

of his ministry, also came and brought a mixture of myrrh and aloes. They took the body of Jesus and wound linen cloth around it with the spices, which was the burial custom of the Jews. Near the place where He was crucified there was a garden, and in the garden there was a new tomb that had never been used. They laid Jesus in it because it was the Jews' day of preparation for the Sabbath and the tomb was nearby. ✝

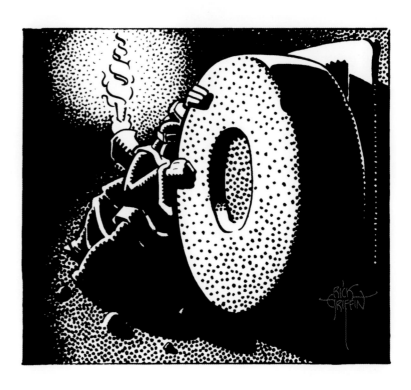

The Most Important Event in History

ON SUNDAY MARY MAGDALENE, PETER, AND JOHN DISCOVER AN EMPTY TOMB ✝ JESUS APPEARS TO MARY, THEN TO THE DISCIPLES IN A LOCKED ROOM
LATER HE AGAIN APPEARS TO THEM AND THOMAS ✝ JESUS AS THE CHRIST, THE SON OF GOD, BRINGS SPIRITUAL LIFE TO THOSE WHO BELIEVE IN HIM

CHAPTER TWENTY

ARLY IN THE MORNING of the first day of the week, when it was still dark, Mary Magdalene went to the tomb. When she saw that the stone had been taken away from the tomb, she ran and found Simon Peter and the other disciple that Jesus loved. Mary said to them, "They have taken the Lord out of the tomb and we do not know where they have placed Him." The two disciples ran together to the tomb but the other disciple outran Peter. When he arrived first at the tomb, he stooped down and looked in and saw the linen cloth laying there, but he didn't go in. However, when Peter arrived, he went into the tomb and saw the linen cloth and the napkin that had been on Jesus' head (which was not lying with the linen cloth but was folded and in a place by itself). Then the other disciple went in, and when he saw, he believed. The disciples did not know the Scriptures which prophesied that He must rise from the dead. Then the disciples went home.

But Mary stood outside of the tomb, weeping, and as she wept she stooped down and looked into the tomb. There she saw two angels in white—one sitting at the head and the other at the foot of where the body of Jesus had been lying. They said to her, "Why are you crying?" She answered them, "Because they have taken away my Lord, and I do not know where they have put Him." When she said this, she turned around and saw Jesus standing there, but she did not know it was Him. Jesus said to her, "Why are you crying? Who are you looking for?" And she, thinking that He was the gardener, said to Him, "Sir, if You have taken Him someplace, just tell me where You've put Him, and I will

Go to My brothers and tell them that I am ascending to My Father
and your Father, and to My God and your God.

The disciples did not know the Scriptures which prophesied that He must rise from the dead. **JOHN 20:9**

take Him away." Jesus said to her, "Mary." She turned and said to Him, "*Rabboni!*" (which means "Master"). Jesus said to her, "Don't cling to Me, for I have not yet ascended to My Father. Go to My brothers and tell them that I am ascending to My Father and your Father, and to My God and your God." Mary Magdalene went and told the disciples that she had seen the Lord and that He had said these things to her.

In the evening of that same day, which was Sunday, the disciples were assembled together in a room with the doors shut, for they feared the Jews. And Jesus came and stood in the midst of them and said, "*Shalom.*" When He had said this, He showed them His hands and His side. The disciples were glad when they saw the Lord. Jesus said to them, "Peace to you; as My Father has sent Me, I also am sending you." When He had said this, He breathed on them and said, "Receive the Holy Spirit. If you forgive someone's sins they have already been forgiven, and if you retain someone's sins they have already been retained."

Thomas, one of the twelve who was called "the Twin," was not with them when Jesus came. Later when they told him, "We have seen the Lord," Thomas said, "Unless I can see His hands and put my finger into the wound made by the nails and place my hand into His side, I will not believe." Eight days later, the disciples were gathered again and Thomas was with them. Jesus came again into the room while the doors were shut and stood in the midst of them and said, "*Shalom.*" Then He said to Thomas, "Touch My hand with your finger and touch My side with your hand, and do not be without faith but believe." Thomas said to Him, "My Lord and My God!" Jesus said to him, "Thomas, because you have seen Me, you believe. Blessed are those who believe, though they have not seen."

Jesus did many other miracles in their presence which were not written in this book, but these were written so that you would believe that Jesus is the Christ, the Son of God, and that by believing you would have life through His name. ✝

Thomas said to Him, My Lord and My God!
Jesus said to him, Thomas, because you have seen Me, you believe.
Blessed are those who believe
though they have not seen.

The Right Side

JESUS STANDS ON THE SHORE WHILE SOME OF THE DISCIPLES FISH FROM A BOAT WITHOUT SUCCESS † HE TELLS THEM WHAT TO DO. AND THEY PULL IN A GREAT
MULTITUDE OF FISH † JESUS HAS A TALK WITH PETER † JOHN CONCLUDES HIS GOSPEL. THOUGH IT IS FAR FROM COMPLETE

CHAPTER TWENTY-ONE

ESUS SHOWED HIMSELF again to the disciples at the Sea of Tiberias, and this is what happened. When Simon Peter, Thomas (who is called "the Twin"), Nathanael (who was of Cana in Galilee), the sons of Zebedee, and two other disciples were together, Simon Peter said to them, "I'm going fishing." The other disciples said, "We'll go with you." They got into a ship and fished all that night but caught nothing.

In the morning, Jesus stood on the shore, but the disciples did not know that it was Him, and Jesus called to them, "Did you catch anything?" They answered Him, "No." He said to them, "Throw out your net on the right side of the ship and you will find them." They threw out their net on the right side and were not able to draw it in, because there were so many fish. When the disciple whom Jesus loved saw that, he said to Peter, "It is the Lord!" When Simon Peter heard that it was the Lord, he threw on his coat (for he was naked) and he dove into the sea and swam to shore. The other

Simon, son of Jonas,
do you love Me with a fervent love?
Peter replied, Yes, Lord, You know that
I am Your friend. He said to him,

Feed My sheep.

They threw out their net on the right side and were not able to draw it in, because there were so many fish. **JOHN 21:6**

disciples came in a small boat, for they were not far from land (about three hundred yards), and they were dragging the net with the fish.

As soon as they reached the shore, they saw a fire with fish lying on it and bread. Jesus said to them, "Bring some of the fish which you have caught." So Simon Peter drew the net to land and it was full with one hundred and fifty-three great fish. Despite the number the net did not break. Jesus said to them, "Come and eat." None of the disciples dared to ask Him, "Who are You?" because they knew that it was the Lord. Jesus then took bread and fish and gave it to them. This was the third time that Jesus showed Himself to His disciples after He had risen from the dead.

After they had eaten, Jesus said to Simon Peter, "Simon, son of Jonas, do you love Me more than these?" Peter answered Him, "Yes, Lord, You know that I am Your friend." Jesus said to him, "Feed My lambs." He said to him again the second time, "Simon, son of Jonas, do you love Me with a fervent love?" Peter replied, "Yes, Lord, You know that I am Your friend." He said to him, "Feed My sheep." Jesus said to him a third time, "Simon, son of Jonas, are you My friend?" Peter was grieved because the third time Jesus asked him, "Are you My friend?" And he answered, "Lord, You know all things, and You know that I am Your friend." Jesus said to him, "Feed My sheep. I tell you the truth, that when you were young, you put on your own clothes and walked where you wanted. But when you are old, your hands will be stretched out by others who will clothe you and take you where you do not want to go." Jesus said this to indicate the kind of death Peter would die in order to glorify God. When He had told him this, He said to him, "Follow Me."

Peter turned around and saw the disciple whom Jesus loved following them (the same disciple who had leaned on Jesus at the supper and had said, "Lord, who is it that is going to betray You?") Then Peter said to Jesus, "Lord, what about him?" Jesus said to Peter, "If I want him to live until I come, what difference does that make to you? Follow Me."

This started a rumor among the believers that John would not die. But Jesus had not said that he would not die, but He said, "If I want him to live until I come, what difference does that make to you?"

I, John, am the disciple who saw and wrote about these things, and I know that this report is true.

There are also many other things which Jesus did, and if every last one were recorded, I suppose that the world itself could not contain all of the books that could be written. Amen. ✝

There are also many other things which Jesus did, and if every last one were recorded, I suppose that the world itself could not contain all of the books that could be written.

AMEN.

He is the creative Force behind everything that has been created. In Him is life and this life is the Light of men. **JOHN 1:3-4**

2,000 Years Later ...What Now?

THE REASON GOD sent Jesus into the world was not to condemn it, but that the world might be saved through Him (John 3:17). God chose to send His Son because only through the blood of a perfect sacrifice could man be redeemed from sin. Jesus tells us, in no uncertain terms, that He is the Messiah promised by the prophets, the Christ, our salvation. Throughout His ministry, signs and miracles demonstrated this truth.

Jesus is approached by Nicodemus (a Pharisee who has come to believe in Jesus) and tells him that unless a man be born again, he cannot see the kingdom of God. Nicodemus queries how it is possible for a man to be born again when he is old. Jesus answers that man must be born twice: of water and the Spirit.

We are told that "All men have sinned, and come short of the glory of God" (Romans 3:23), and that as sinners, our spirits are condemned to die. "For the wages of sin is death" (Romans 6:23); "Sin brings forth death" (James 1:15). We must accept by an act of faith that His purpose was to defeat death. He died for our sins, as He had promised, and then rose the third day, visibly demonstrating His power over death.

To be born again is an act of faith—a matter of believing within our spirit that what was accomplished by Jesus was accomplished for all men. "Believe in the Lord Jesus Christ, and thou shalt be saved, and thy house" (Acts 16:31).

If you wish to become a new believer, pray; call upon the Lord. Repent, ask for forgiveness of sin. As the tax collector in Luke 16 demonstrated, pray, "God, be merciful to me a sinner," and your new life will begin. Know that your new life has begun because God promises: "For whosoever shall call upon the name of the Lord, shall be saved" (Romans 10:13).

You may not feel any change. Don't trust your feelings because they change. Trust God's unchanging promises. Remember that you will be a baby for a while. You may fall at times, but you will grow. The Holy Spirit will be teaching you, changing and perfecting you (2 Corinthians 3:18).

The Next Step
4 important things to grow

1.] PRAY EVERY DAY.

Let the Holy Spirit show you how to talk to God. Pray in the name of Jesus Christ (read John 14:13). Listen for what God might have to tell you (Revelation 3:22).

2.] SHARE YOUR FAITH.

Tell others what has happened to you. Be baptized and participate in communion (Acts 2:42). As God begins working in your life, you will find joy in sharing your faith with others.

3.] READ THE BIBLE.

This is the primary way God has of communicating with you. It is absolutely essential. Your physical body needs food and so does your spirit. The Bible is spiritual food (2 Peter 3:18).

4.] BE WITH OTHER CHRISTIANS.

As much as possible, fellowship with people whose lives have been changed as yours has (1 John 1:3, Hebrews 10:25). If you do not know of a group of believers with whom you can identify, pray and ask the Lord to show you the right place to go.

If you are unsure after that, contact:

THE WORD FOR TODAY
P.O. Box 8000
Costa Mesa, CA 92628
Website: twft.com
E-mail: info@twft.com
1-800-272-WORD (9673)

Chuck Smith
Seasoned with Grace

by Chuck Smith Jr.

I TREASURE **a memory** of Dad that, to me, characterizes his constant enthusiasm and profound gratitude during the period of Calvary Chapel's explosive growth. Prior to the Jesus Movement, no one expected Calvary Chapel to become a mega-church. For example, when we were finally in a position to construct our own building from the ground up, it proved to be pathetically inadequate to accommodate the ever-increasing crowds from our very first service in it.

At one point, we were caught in transition after selling one property in order to purchase another. Calvary Chapel was going to be homeless for several months. That challenge resulted in the season of "The Tent," a rented "big-top" large enough to host a three-ring circus. Some people wondered whether the church needed so much extra space (maximum seating in the tent was 2,000 and the number of people who could crowd into the three services at our previous facility was about 1,200). But attendance continued to swell until we were forced to add a second Sunday morning service, and then only a few months later we added a third. Even then, the tent panels were removed each weekend so that people sitting outside could feel included in the meetings.

One night, after church was over, Dad and I walked from the tent alone toward the parking lot. In those days, he always lingered to talk with people, hear about the most recent miracle, and pray for anyone who poured out their troubles to him. Before reaching the car, Dad stopped, turned around, and looked back towards the tent. As I recall, a full moon was shining above the silhouette of the three large posts on which the canopy was suspended, which in the imagination of a few hippies stood as symbols of the Trinity.

Dad sighed and it seemed like we were on the verge of one of those father-son moments. "Could you have ever guessed," he wondered aloud, "that God was going to do a work like this and that He would choose to use us?" I said, "No," shook my head, and remember only that whatever else I said was lame. But Dad did not notice; his mind was wandering down his own sublime path and he was obviously savoring the moment. "Who could ever comprehend the grace of God or how it would work in our lives?"

Some Christians are naturally curious about their leaders, whether they are the same person offstage as they are onstage. Do pastors and evangelists act the same way at home with their family as they

do when in front of an audience? I have always found pleasure in the genuineness of Dad's faith and that everything he says about God's grace, he fully believes and practices. In fact, there is no other doctrine or attribute of God that so well complements Dad's positive and optimistic personality as the grace and graciousness of God.

I must admit, however, that I do not remember the theme of grace being as predominant in Dad's ministry prior to the onslaught of hippies to our church. Of course, it is altogether possible that I had not been paying close attention to his teaching previously, but I do believe that he had a lot more to say about grace and he said it more often after we were dubbed "the hippie church." At the same time, Dad faced sharp criticism for welcoming into his church refugees from the counter-culture who came bearded, barefoot and braless.

A few months ago I asked Dad when he first started to take God's grace so seriously. I had guessed that he picked it up while teaching the book of Romans in the tent during the early seventies. I was half-right. Dad said that when we lived in Huntington Beach (late 1950s) he taught through Romans for the first time. One of the Bible commentaries he studied was William Newell's. There he found an endnote following chapter six entitled, "A Few Words About Grace." The light came on. Dad realized there was nothing he had to do to earn, produce, or trigger God's grace, but that it was operative in his daily life simply because it pleases God to be gracious. From that moment on, Dad was convinced he could greet each new day with the most hopeful expectations, even if he did not deserve to receive one good thing from God.

Dad has said, "I expect God to give me a blessing everyday." I can only say that I wish I had inherited more of his positive genes. I have witnessed a long chain of blessings in Dad's life, linking one day to the next, one decision to the next, one transaction to the next. His faith in God's goodness is absolute. Dad sets out every day with the intent, not to impress God, but to enjoy Him. He does not try to prove himself to God, but rejoices at the way God proves Himself to him.

Most importantly, however, Dad has learned to extend God's grace to others, even people who have received help from him and then turned on him. But Dad needed an understanding of grace and a strong commitment to establish his life on it in order to be available to love the thousands of confused children who found their way from the drug houses of Southern California to the house of God. Upon entering the open doors of Calvary Chapel, they received the warm welcome of this husky man, the instant affection of his tender heart, and the encouragement of his smile as radiant and broad as the grace of God. †

Rick Griffin
Creating with New Vision

by Gordon T. McClelland

IN THE MID 1970s Calvary Chapel of Costa Mesa was exploding with creative energy. Some of the hippies that got saved during the Jesus People Movement were visual artists and musicians. As they grew in their faith, many began seeking ways to glorify God through their art and music. From the very beginning, Pastor Chuck Smith recognized these gifts and encouraged the artists and musicians to seek God for direction in developing their talents. In addition, the church often helped finance projects when it came to practical application.

Chuck Smith's priority as pastor of the church was to teach the Word of God. His messages consistently proclaimed God's love, which resonated strongly with a generation of people who were seeking to live a love-filled life. He found the gospel of John especially helpful in bringing the true message of love to them. On many occasions he directed new Christians to study the gospel of John and also suggested they use those Scriptures when witnessing to unbelieving friends.

During this period, Chuck Fromm was involved with Christian music projects, outreach programs and publishing. Many of his projects were affiliated with Calvary Chapel. While working on one of these projects, he met Rick Griffin, a talented and innovative artist. In California hippie and surf culture circles, Griffin was quite famous. Throughout the early 1960s he created a cartoon strip featuring the character Murphy. This cartoon strip was published regularly in *Surfer Magazine*, which was the main publication for the California-Hawaiian surf culture.

In the late 1960s Rick lived in San Francisco and created art for a number of rock music bands including the Jimi Hendrix Experience, Quicksilver Messenger Service, Big Brother and the Holding Company and the Grateful Dead. Millions of posters and record covers designed by Griffin were printed and distributed worldwide.

By 1970 Rick had received Jesus Christ as his Savior and was walking with the Lord. The Griffin family was living in San Clemente and fellowshiping at a local Baptist church. At this time Rick and fellow artist Craig Yoe had a series of discussions about developing an illustrated version of the gospel of John, but it never developed into a publishing project.

About this same time Rick became friends with Greg Laurie, who at the time was producing Christian tracts and cartoons. Greg was excited about Rick becoming a Christian and invited him to attend services at Calvary Chapel. A few years later he met Oden Fong and Lewis McVay, also from Calvary Chapel. They had a band named Mustard Seed Faith and asked Rick to paint a picture for use on the cover of their album titled *Sail On Sailor*.

Rick accepted this job and came up with an image of a sailing ship with heaven in the clouds. This quickly became a popular Christian image. Chuck Fromm was impressed with this record cover and immediately asked Rick if he would be interested in illustrating the gospel of John. Chuck Smith would write the paraphrased text and Rick would do the illustrations.

Rick was interested and told Fromm about his previous desire to do this type of project. The problem was that Rick wasn't in any position to take the assignment. At that moment in time, his car was broken down and the landlord had asked him to move out of the house he was renting in San Clemente. Fromm offered to help Rick resolve these problems. As it turned out, he arranged for Rick and his family to move into an apartment in Santa Ana, across from Calvary Chapel. He also arranged to get them a new car.

photo courtesy of Art Brewer

In addition, Fromm located studio space for Rick and arranged for him to receive a regular paycheck. This was truly a blessing for the Griffin family, which included Rick's wife, Ida, and their two daughters, Flaven and Adelia. Two more children named Miles and Katie would soon be added to the Griffin family while Rick was working on illustrations for *The Gospel of John*.

When Rick committed to something, he went all the way. That was just his personality. He prayed and studied the gospel of John over and over. In addition he listened to Chuck Smith's Bible tapes and read what other pastors and theologians wrote about the book of John. After about a month he began serious work on the illustrations.

At first he produced a series of black-and-white illustrations. Most were done with pen and ink on board. Some of these depict specific Bible stories and others were graphic images designed around numbers for chapter headings. Sometimes after finishing a work, he would get another picture in his mind. Often he would produce a second or even third image to illustrate a single idea. That is why finished original art from *The Gospel of John* project with variations and different images turned up from time to time.

Chapter one was one of the first works he produced for the project. His visual interpretation of "In the beginning …" was a series of floating planet-like spheres. The number "1" forms a doorway with a blinding light behind it. Jesus, dressed as the Good Shepherd is walking through the door and toward the viewer. After completing this work of art, Rick began thinking about interesting ways to use the chapter numbers as part of a picture or spot illustration.

Anyone that knew Rick well was aware of his playful sense of humor. Whenever you would see that suspicious smile and a twinkle in his eye, you knew that he was up to something. In chapter five he picked out verse 8 where Jesus tells the man to take up his bed and walk. Rick used the "keep on truckin" man stepping through the number "5" and holding a full-size bed over his head. Rick was thoroughly amused when he thought this one up and enjoyed showing the art to friends.

For chapter nine he chose verse 11 where Jesus healed the blind man. This one features two-winged eyeballs standing next to the number 9. Eyeball images appeared in many of Rick's works of art both before and after he became a Christian. Originally it came from hot rod art he saw as a kid in the 1950s. The image stuck with him and in some ways it became a sort of trademark character for Rick.

Rick's art studio was located on MacArthur Boulevard in Santa Ana. It was filled with all sorts of stuff including easels, a large light table, stretched canvases and spotlights. Paint tubes, brushes, inking pens and bottles of ink were fanned out on makeshift wooden tables. They blended in with a large indoor palm tree, surfboards, drums, an electric guitar with amp, and thriftstore tables and chairs. Mexican serapes and Indian blankets were draped over furniture. Old advertising signs, books and record albums were on shelves. Piles of sketches on vellum tracing paper stacked up on the floor around his drawing table.

When Rick focused on producing art he often worked 18 to 20 hours straight. He would take catnaps and work steadily like this for several weeks. In between work sessions he would relax, study the Scriptures and talk with people about the Bible verses. Once he formulated some new ideas for art, he would go back on a work schedule.

All of us marveled at his ability to come up with such unique ideas and ink them with such amazing skill. He was not as easily impressed. After being complimented on a work of art he would often say, "Well, it's OK but you should see the way it looks up here (pointing to his mind) … if I could only get that down."

As *The Gospel of John* project began to come into focus he decided to paint a series of largescale works using acrylic paint on stretched canvas. Rick was interested in the art produced by great American illustrators of the 1920s and 1930s and was particularly interested in those who illustrated the classic children's books. Several of the paintings were a sort of tribute to those artists and their art. Rick would develop his own visual imagery but would appropriate just enough of an idea or painting technique from one of these artists so it could be recognized by those very familiar with the old-time illustrators' work. It was a sort of fun game Rick would play.

When he painted John the Baptist on the hill above a valley, it was a tip of the hat to artist N.C. Wyeth. The idea of having a face or figure appear in the clouds was successfully developed by Wyeth and was used several times on bookcover illustrations in the 1920s. The face of Jesus appears in the clouds in Rick's painting. The portrait of John the Baptist on the lefthand side of the painting looks a lot like a picture of Rick. He really liked the character of John the Baptist in the Scriptures and thought they shared the common commitment to point people to salvation in Jesus.

The Hosanna painting features the triumphal entry of Jesus into Jerusalem. This painting was inspired by the art of Dean Cornwell. On first look it appears this painting depicts the New Testament era, but on closer inspection people from all periods of time and places can be seen. On the right side is a 1920s Spanish dancing girl and Rick's wife, Ida, holding her new baby, Katie. Rick himself appears with a staff in hand and a small surfer boy holding a skateboard is to the left of Jesus. If you look really close you will see that on the boy's shirt is written Lynard Skynard. The night Rick was painting the depiction of the boy, a radio program announced that an airplane had just crashed, killing several members of that rock band. This was sort of a prayer for them.

The composition and general idea for the crucifixion was inspired by calendar art of the 1940s. The contemporary man is reading his Bible and in his mind he sees the picture above his head. The crucifix is in the center of the man's thought dream and the two thieves are on each side. Behind the crucifix is the tree of life and a backlit doorway. The only way to the other side of this narrow doorway is through the finished work of Jesus Christ on the cross and the shedding of His blood.

While Rick was right in the middle of this project he was told that Bob Dylan was attending church and was interested in Christianity. The piece he was working on at the time pictured a young man stepping out of a circle and moving from his old life with a dark past into a new life in Christ. This was to represent the idea of being born again. Rick was a big fan of Dylan's writing and music. He made the young man to look a bit like Dylan in hopes that what he heard was true. This image was also used on a flyer to advertise the Saturday night youth gatherings at Calvary Chapel.

After about two and a half years of starts and stops, a preliminary version of *The Gospel of John* was published. It was printed in a large format on newsprint paper. The response was very good. Rick continued to work on several more illustrations, while another artist Kerne Erickson worked on designing a smaller, more colorful version. The final publication came out in the early 1980s. It was 8 1/2 x 11 inches, printed on slick paper and was published in a staple-bound booklet format. Many thousands of these *The Gospel of John* booklets were distributed on an international level.

It was truly a blessing to have worked closely with Rick Griffin and Chuck Fromm on *The Gospel of John* project. Since the mid 1970s I have regularly attended services at Calvary Chapel and consider Chuck Smith to be my pastor. Rick Griffin was a close friend and his Christian testimony strongly influenced me to seek redemption through Jesus Christ.

I can attest to the fact that in the 1970s Chuck Smith and Rick Griffin were very different people, in almost every way. The common bond was that they were both committed to serving God and proclaiming the love of Jesus Christ to the world. They overlooked the superficial differences, combined their gifts, and focused on what really matters. In many ways this reflects the bigger picture of what was happening at Calvary Chapel during that era and serves to remind us of the fruitful results of putting God and the proclamation of His Word first. ✝